942.31

eb.
Sub.

Wiltshire Record Society

(formerly the Records Branch of the Wiltshire
Archaeological and Natural History Society)

VOLUME XXXII
FOR THE YEAR 1976

Impression of 425 copies

THE SUBSCRIPTION BOOK OF BISHOPS

TOUNSON AND DAVENANT

1620–40

EDITED BY

BARRIE WILLIAMS

DEVIZES
1977

Set in Times New Roman 10/11 pt.

PRINTED IN ENGLAND BY
WARWICK PRINTING COMPANY LTD.
WARWICK

CONTENTS

PREFACE

Work on this volume began under the guidance of Mr. C. R. Elrington, honorary editor of the Society 1962–72, and was completed under that of Dr. D. A. Crowley, honorary editor 1972–6. The editor of the volume, Mr. Williams, wishes to thank them for their advice and encouragement. Warm thanks are also extended to Mr. P. V. McGrath of the University of Bristol, who first suggested an edition of the subscription book, to Miss K. Pamela Stewart and the staff of the Salisbury Diocesan Record Office, and to Mr. R. A. Read of the Salisbury Diocesan Registry. The subscription book is published by permission of the Diocesan Registrar.

Generalizations about the clergy in the period preceding the Civil Wars must be tested against such a body of facts as Mr. Williams has provided in this edition. Here is material for investigation of the social standing, education, and personal connexions of hundreds of individuals in a considerable part of western England. Historians engaged in current debates on the early-Stuart church have cause to join with members of this Society in their thanks to Mr. Williams for his pains.

15 *November* 1976   D. C. Cox

ABBREVIATIONS

AC   J. Venn and J. A. Venn, *Alumni Cantabrigienses*, pt. 1 (1922–7)

ACO   *AC* and *AO*

AO   Joseph Foster, *Alumni Oxonienses* (1891–2)

Conc. Test.   *The concurrent testimony of the ministers in . . . Wiltes with their . . . brethren . . . of London to the truth of Jesus Christ and to the Solemn League and Covenant* (London 1648)

CR   A. G. Matthews, *Calamy revised* (1934)

DNB   L. Stephen and S. Lee (eds.), *Dictionary of national biography* (1885–1900)

FS   W. H. R. Jones, *Fasti ecclesiae Sarisberiensis* (1879)

PR   T. Phillipps, *Institutiones clericorum in comitatu Wiltoniae* (1825)

WR   A. G. Matthews, *Walker revised* (1948)

INTRODUCTION

SUBSCRIPTION TO THE THIRTY-NINE ARTICLES

The Thirty-nine Articles of Religion were drawn up by Convocation in 1563.[1] Although from the start they carried weight as a statement of the doctrine of the Church of England, it was only gradually that all clergy were required to subscribe to them. Until 1571 only members of Convocation had to do so. In that year, however, after the excommunication and deposition of Queen Elizabeth by Pope Pius V, an Act was passed to require clergy under the degree of bishop ordained in Mary's reign to subscribe 'to all the articles of religion which only concern the confession of the true Christian faith and the doctrine of the sacraments'.[2] The Act distinguished between those doctrinal articles, which were more of a test to the Romanists, and the disciplinary articles, which were more of a test to the Puritans. Parliament was more sympathetic to the Puritans and did not demand subscription to the disciplinary articles. In 1571, however, Convocation on its own authority, but with the backing of the queen who refused to submit the articles to Parliament's approval, required subscription to all the articles by all the Marian clergy except bishops.[3] Subscription to all the articles has never been demanded by statute.

In 1583 Archbishop Whitgift drew up articles to which preachers were obliged to consent and subscribe.[4] They contained within them, besides acknowledgement of the royal supremacy and the authority of the Book of Common Prayer, allowance of the articles of 1563. Whitgift's articles were primarily intended to enforce conformity on those with Puritan inclinations but in attempting that they extended subscription to the Thirty-nine Articles to all clergymen. It is not clear how far subscription to Whitgift's articles was enforced but the articles were an important step towards the general subscription to the Thirty-nine Articles enforced after 1604. In that year the canons of the Church of England were thoroughly revised. Canon 36 provided that every man to be received into the ministry or admitted to an ecclesiastical living had to make and subscribe to a declaration affirming Whitgift's articles.[5] Before a man might preach, catechize, or be a Lecturer or Reader of Divinity in either university he had to be licensed and to subscribe. Licences could be granted and subscriptions taken by the archbishop,

---

[1] The articles are printed in the Book of Common Prayer.
[2] *Church Acts and Measures* (Church Assembly), 327–8.
[3] E. J. Bicknell, *Thirty-Nine Articles*, 20–1.
[4] The articles are printed in *Select Statutes and other Constitutional Documents*, ed. G. W. Prothero, 211–12.
[5] *Constitutions and Canons Ecclesiastical of the Church of England*, ed. M. E. C. Walcott, 22–3.

the bishop of the diocese where the man was to be placed, or one of the universities. The declaration had to be made in the presence of the bishop of the diocese in which the clergyman was to serve.[1] The exact form of the declaration was laid down: 'I A.B. do willingly and *ex animo* subscribe to these three articles . . . and to all things that are contained in them'.[2] Despite the careful wording of the canon, however, the form varied in practice. That used in Salisbury diocese is given below.[3]

The canon law on subscription to the Thirty-nine Articles has been very little changed since 1604. The Puritan party was not entirely satisfied with the articles themselves and in 1604 an unsuccessful attempt to have them amended was made at the Hampton Court Conference. In 1628 Charles I gave them added authority by prefixing the royal declaration. In 1643 the Westminster Assembly appointed a committee to amend the articles and article 16, on Pre-destination, was revised in a more definitely Calvinistic direction, but during the Civil War and Interregnum they were not abolished. The procedure for subscribing to them lapsed of course and subscription to more recent declarations, especially the Solemn League and Covenant, became more important. The Restoration brought back the 1604 requirement of subscription but in 1660–1 the Puritans again pressed, without success, for amendment of the articles. The articles of 1563 still stand and subscription by all clergymen as laid down in 1604 is still required, although since 1865 a more general form of subscription has replaced specific assent to each article.[4]

In the early 17th century a candidate for holy orders, a benefice, or a licence to preach was required to make a number of oaths and declarations. Besides assenting to the articles, which he had to do before the bishop orally and by subscription, he took the traditional oath of canonical obedience to the bishop of the diocese. The 1559 Act of Supremacy required him to take an oath to the sovereign as Supreme Governor of the Church. An Act of 1563 required him to take an oath against the authority, jurisdiction, and power of the Pope. The 1604 canons required candidates for benefices to declare against simony.

SUBSCRIPTION IN SALISBURY DIOCESE

The Ordination of Ministers Act of 1571 required the bishop to issue a testimonial of subscription to the articles.[5] It was obviously convenient that a bishop should keep a register of subscriptions but such a record was not required by canon or statute and no record of subscriptions in the ordinary

[1] Ibid. 23–4. The canon does not lay down the procedure to be followed in the case of university subscriptions.
[2] Bicknell, *Thirty-Nine Articles*, 20.
[3] See p. 7.
[4] A full summary of the history of the Thirty-nine Articles is given in Bicknell, *Thirty-Nine Articles*, 7–21.
[5] *Church Acts and Measures* (Church Assembly), 328.

jurisdiction of the bishop is known in the diocese of Salisbury before 1620. The book begun then, which is edited below, records subscriptions to the Thirty-nine Articles made between 1620 and 1640 on appointments to benefices, admissions to holy orders, and the receiving of licences to preach. The 1604 canons required schoolmasters to subscribe before receiving a licence from the bishop to teach[1] but subscription before the bishop of only one (no. 372) is recorded. An Act of 1511 required physicians and surgeons to be examined and licensed by the bishop[2] but again subscription before the bishop of only one physician licensed to practise medicine (no. 814) is recorded. In their exercise of peculiar jurisdiction deans of Salisbury took subscriptions and a book of subscriptions made before them 1599–1673 exists.[3] It records subscriptions in the peculiars of the dean, dean and chapter, and individual prebendaries of the chapter, and in those such as Little Bedwyn (the lord warden of Savernake forest) and Shalbourne (the dean and canons of Windsor) under other jurisdictions. Whereas the bishops' book covers Salisbury diocese, with a few curates from other dioceses, the deans' therefore deals with livings over a wide and scattered area. Those of schoolmasters and physicians were a greater proportion of the subscriptions recorded before the dean than of those before the bishop,[4] suggesting either that the deans were more conscientious than the bishops in licensing them or that the bishop failed to record their subscriptions or recorded them in a separate book which has failed to survive. The deans' book has not been edited but where a man named in the bishops' book, or in the related documents edited below,[5] subscribed before the dean that fact is noted.

Subscriptions by men appointed to benefices are some forty per cent of those recorded in the bishops' book. They were taken at all times of the year and on any day of the week, but frequently on the same day as institution. Sometimes, however, institution apparently preceded subscription.

The next most numerous class of subscribers was those admitted to holy orders, some thirty per cent. To avoid the medieval scandal of 'hedge-priests' with no adequate living to support them the 1604 canons required candidates for ordination, except Fellows of colleges at Oxford and Cambridge, chaplains, or masters of arts of five years' standing living of their own charge, to have a preferment or curacy. A bishop who ordained a candidate not so provided had to maintain him until a living was found. When subscribing before the bishop of Salisbury many candidates for ordination therefore named the curacy to which they had been appointed. Nearly all the remainder may be assumed to have been at the universities. The 1604 canons also laid down that ordinations were to take place on the Sundays following the Ember weeks. That procedure was generally followed in Salisbury diocese. Subscriptions were made either on the day before

---

[1] *Constitutions and Canons Ecclesiastical*, ed. Walcott, 43.
[2] R. Phillimore, *Ecclesiastical Law of the Church of England*, ii. 1635.
[3] In Salisbury Diocesan Record Office.
[4] In the period covered by the bishops' book, 1620–40, 20 schoolmasters and 2 physicians subscribed before the deans.
[5] See pp. 11–12.

ordination or more usually on the day of the ordination itself although at the Michaelmas ordination of 1626 seven subscriptions were made on the Saturday and only one on the Sunday. At Christmas 1631, for example, there were three subscriptions on the Saturday and four on the Sunday. At Michaelmas 1628, however, a candidate subscribed on the Monday following the ordination (no. 310). That was certainly contrary to canon 36 of 1604 but, as candidates wrote out their own subscriptions, it is possible that sometimes differences in the dates given by the candidates when subscribing arose from mistakes. The number of candidates at ordinations shows that in Salisbury diocese a steady stream of men was coming forward for the ministry. The largest number of men at an ordination between 1620 and 1640 was 21, nine priests and twelve deacons, at Advent 1633, and eight priests and thirteen deacons at Trinity 1638. The number ordained at Advent 1633 may have been so large because there had been no Michaelmas ordination that year. There were totals of 26 candidates at Michaelmas and Advent 1622, but since there were no ordinations in the diocese between March 1621 and June 1622 there was still perhaps a back-log to work off. The smallest number of candidates at a canonical season was three, at Lent 1630 and Lent 1635, but Tounson once and Davenant twice held ordinations for single candidates. The ordination of Richard Heighmore (no. 354) on 9 July 1629 was possibly to enable him to serve the cure of Clifton Maybank (Dorset) without delay, but the other two candidates (nos. 46, 699) were men from Oxford University and it is not clear why ordinations were held for them alone. The three subscriptions were made on a Monday, a Thursday, and a Friday suggesting that the canon demanding Sunday ordination could be ignored. The 62 remaining ordinations held by Tounson and Davenant took place at the Ember seasons. The bishops of Salisbury ordained not only candidates from their own diocese and from Oxford University but also from other dioceses. Such 'foreign' candidates often held livings in Dorset, which lay much nearer to Salisbury than their own cathedral church at Bristol. At Michaelmas 1636 seven Dorset ministers, an unusually high number, were ordained at Salisbury because the see of Bristol was vacant. Other subscribers held livings in Winchester diocese, especially in Hampshire, and a few in Gloucester diocese. Ordination only at the four canonical seasons was required partly so that a minimum of a quarter was spent by a deacon before proceeding to the priesthood and the 1604 canons required that the diaconate should normally last a year. In Salisbury diocese that canonical requirement was widely ignored. On the one hand a candidate ordained deacon at one season might receive priest's orders at the next, especially if he was already an incumbent, and on the other hand some of the clergy remained in deacon's orders for several years before proceeding to the priesthood. In the early 17th century a deacon could discharge all the normal duties of a curate. He could preach, visit, catechize, baptize, bury, and marry. The chief duty he could not perform was to celebrate Holy Communion, but in country parishes where Communion was celebrated only quarterly that may not have been a serious impediment. Dons or curates ordained deacon might therefore have had no need to proceed to priest's orders for several years or even at all.

The sacred ministry thus followed a different pattern from that familiar to us in the last hundred years, in which a year in the diaconate has become normal.

Licences to members of the clergy to preach were sometimes granted in batches. In October and November 1620 Bishop Tounson licensed a total of fifteen preachers. Bishop Davenant licensed fourteen in October 1622, in April and May 1631 he licensed ten, between May and July 1635 he licensed seven, and in May and July 1638 he licensed ten. At other times Davenant licensed a steady stream of individual preachers. The licensing of preachers was one of the bishop's most serious responsibilities. The Puritan party regarded the pulpit as their greatest weapon and neither Elizabeth I nor Archbishop Laud was prepared to allow them unrestricted use of it. A strict policy of licensing preachers was therefore introduced by the former and revived by the latter. Only those duly licensed were allowed to preach, other clergy being restricted to reading from the Books of Homilies. The incumbent of a benefice, particularly if he was a graduate, would normally be licensed to preach, at least in his own church, but such permission was not automatic and a licence could be revoked. Permission to preach outside the licencee's own parish, or in the diocese in general, was more sparingly given, and such licences were an indication that the recipient was both competent and orthodox.[1] It is understandable that both Tounson and Davenant should have licensed a large group of preachers early in their episcopates since there was probably a back-log to be made up and it was important that the diocese should have an adequate number of licensed preachers. It is not apparent, however, why Davenant should again have licensed large groups in 1631, 1635, and 1638, unless they were the result of periodic reviews of preaching in the diocese, possibly arising from his visitations. There is no evidence that either Tounson or Davenant licensed or refused to license clergy of a particular party or that the licensed preachers were diligent or otherwise in preaching.

THE SUBSCRIPTION BOOK

Subscriptions before Bishops Tounson and Davenant are contained in a single bound volume. The book, which was repaired in 1952, has 235 numbered folios and measures approximately $7\frac{3}{4}$ ins. by $6\frac{1}{2}$ ins. by 2 ins. Its cover bears no title, nor do its two constituent parts within, but a title page has been written at a later date. It reads 'Subscription Book Vol. I 1620 to 1671. N.B. The earliest entries are at the end of the Book'. That page draws attention to the fact that the entries for Tounson's episcopate are at the end of the book, on folios 223–32. It is not clear why so much of the book was at first left blank. It was presumably intended for some other

[1] J. R. H. Moorman, *History of the Church in England*, 219; Owen Chadwick, *Reformation*, 417 ff.; Carl Bridenbaugh, *Vexed and Troubled Englishmen 1590–1642*, 293–300; H. R. Trevor-Roper, *Archbishop Laud*, 106–7, 111–12.

purpose, perhaps to list the clergy of the diocese already ordained and instituted, but the pages remained blank while Tounson was bishop. The last subscription of his episcopate made two days before his death is recorded on the third folio from the end of the book. Subscriptions in Davenant's episcopate are recorded at the front of the book. Those from 18 November 1621 to 5 August 1640, the date of the last recorded subscription before the Civil War, occupy folios 27–210. No further subscription in the diocese is recorded before 1664. The title page also implies the existence of a second subscription book, that now covering the years 1664–8.[1] The gap in the records from 1640 to 1660 can be explained by the Civil War, Commonwealth, and Protectorate, but the lack of records for the post-Restoration episcopates of Duppa, Henchman, and part of that of Earle cannot be explained. Three later subscriptions are recorded at the end of Tounson's and Davenant's book, those of a physician licensed in 1669 to practise medicine and of two ordinands who probably subscribed at Michaelmas 1671. They appear immediately after the last subscription of 1640. It is not clear how they came to be there but they have been abstracted and printed below along with the other subscriptions.

The book contains a recital of various oaths (ff. 6–11), a copy of the Thirty-nine Articles printed in London by Robert Barker, printer to the king, in 1612 which is bound into the book (ff. 15–26), subscriptions before Davenant (ff. 27–210), the subscriptions of 1669 and 1671 (f. 210), and subscriptions before Tounson (ff. 223–32). The oaths are the oath of supremacy required by the Act of 1559 (f. 6), the declaration against the power and jurisdiction of the Pope required by the Act of 1563 (f. 7), the oath of allegiance and supremacy required by the Act of 1606 (ff. 8–9),[2] the oath against simony (f. 9),[3] the oath of canonical obedience to the bishop of the diocese and his successors (f. 10), and the threefold oath affirming the royal supremacy, the Prayer Book and Ordinal, and the Thirty-nine Articles drawn up by Whitgift in 1583 and re-affirmed by the canons of 1604 (f. 11). Some of the folios on which they are recited have been damaged at the top but the full texts can be reconstructed from the remaining part. The oaths, all well known, and the Thirty-nine Articles have not been reproduced below and the subscriptions before Tounson and Davenant have been taken in the reverse order from that in which they appear in the original. Some of the folios on which the sub-scriptions are recorded have also been partly damaged, mostly on the right-hand side or at the foot, but it has usually been possible to reconstruct or deduce the entry and footnotes indicate where that has been done. Some of the sections are separated by folios, otherwise blank, on some of which short notes were made in Davenant's time. A few are worth mentioning. Notes were made, for example, that no one was to be admitted to the vicarage of Chieveley (Berks.) before Arthur Oade, gentleman, or Thomas Shuter, his proctor, were called, and, more succinctly, 'Mr. Place for Letcom

[1] In Salisbury Diocesan Record Office.
[2] This was an oath which the bishop was empowered to administer to suspected papists. It was not administered to Anglican clergy.
[3] The only one of the oaths for which there is a heading in the subscription book.

Basset' and 'Remember Crolee for Doctor Hincman' (f. 222). 'Place' may be John Place (no. 101), vicar of Denchworth (Berks.). Dr. Hincman is Humphrey Henchman (no. 125), then a prebendary and afterwards bishop of Salisbury. Crolee has not been identified.

The 1604 canons required a candidate for holy orders to have taken a degree or 'at the least . . . be able to yield an account of his faith in Latin'.[1] At subscription, therefore, incumbents and preachers usually specified their degree and candidates for holy orders usually specified in addition the college at which they had graduated. If non-graduates the subscribers described themselves as learned in Latin or specified a college at which they had studied. The subscriptions were all made in Latin. In the deans' book, however, fourteen subscriptions were made in English in the period 1620–40, most by schoolmasters who were not graduates although in 1634 two graduate curates subscribed in English. The form of words used was the same whether in Latin or English. A typical subscription from the bishops' book for a candidate for a benefice (no. 1) reads 'Ego Thomas Lloyd clericus in artibus magister admittendus et instituendus ad officium vicariam de Woton Basset in Comitatu Wilts. Sarum diocesie omnibus his[2] articulis et singulis in eisdem contentis volens et ex animo subscribo et consensum meum eisdem prebo. Tertiodecimo die Julii 1620. Thomas Lloyd.' For a candidate for holy orders a typical subscription (no. 8) reads 'Ego Johannes Singleton in artibus baccelaureus e Collegio Reginae Oxoniensis iam diaconus et nunc in officium presbyteri admittendus omnibus hisce articulis . . . '. The fact that all candidates for the priesthood were already deacons was a result of the 1604 canons which forbade ordination as deacon and priest on the same day,[3] a medieval practice regarded as an abuse by the Protestant reformers because it reduced the importance of the diaconate. A typical subscription on receiving a licence to preach (no. 32) reads 'Ego Antonius White clericus in artibus magister licentiandus ad praedicandum et exponendum verbum Dei in quacunque ecclesia infra diocesiam Sarum omnibus hisce articulis . . . '. Sometimes (e.g. no. 20) the licence to preach was not a general one for the diocese but a specific one for a particular church or for a church and neighbouring churches. Those forms of subscription differed, but not significantly, from that laid down in 1604[4] and from that most widely used: 'I A.B. do willingly and from my heart subscribe to the Thirty-nine Articles of Religion of the United Church of England and Ireland, and to the three articles in the 30th canon, and to all things therein contained'.[5]

[1] *Constitutions and Canons Ecclesiastical*, ed. Walcott, canon 34.
[2] The form 'hisce' was often used.
[3] *Constitutions and Canons Ecclesiastical*, ed. Walcott, canon 32.
[4] See p. 2.
[5] Bicknell, *Thirty-Nine Articles*, 20–1.

THE BISHOPS

Robert Tounson[1] is not among the best remembered bishops of Salisbury. After graduating at Queens' College, Cambridge, in 1592 at the age of seventeen he was beneficed in the Peterborough diocese. In 1604 he was instituted as vicar of Wellingborough (Northants.) and in 1606 was presented to the rectory of Old (Northants.) which he retained until his promotion to Salisbury. He attracted the favour of James I and became a royal chaplain and in 1617 dean of Westminster. He was consecrated bishop of Salisbury on 9 July 1620. He died on 15 May 1621, aged 46, having been bishop only ten months. Tounson who had married in 1604, and had fifteen children by, Margaret Davenant, daughter of a London merchant, died 'in a mean condition'[2] leaving his large family in straitened circumstances. The 53 recorded subscriptions before him coincide almost exactly with his episcopate, the first entry made 13 July 1620, four days after his consecration, the last 13 May 1621, two days before his death. His widow was ejected by the dean and chapter of Westminster from the Curate's House at St. Margaret's, Westminster, in 1624.[3] She died in 1634 and was buried in Salisbury cathedral. By the time of her death several of her children had begun to prosper.[4] Tounson was succeeded as bishop by his brother-in-law John Davenant. Born in 1576, only a year after Tounson, Davenant survived him by twenty years. He too was a graduate of Queens' College, Cambridge, but unlike Tounson followed an academic career.[5]   From 1609 to 1621 he was Lady Margaret Professor of Divinity at Cambridge and from 1614 Master of Queens' College. In 1618 he was one of the representatives of the Church of England at the Synod of Dort and his part at the synod, at which he upheld a moderate Calvinistic line, brought him into favour with James I. As a result he was consecrated bishop of Salisbury in 1621. In choosing him for Salisbury the king is said to have been partly influenced by the fact that Davenant was a bachelor, hoping that, having no family of his own, he might take from the Church the burden of supporting Tounson's many children.[6] During his episcopate a number of Davenant's relatives received promotion in the Salisbury diocese. In 1622 he presented Thomas Fuller, the husband of his sister Judith, to the prebend of Highworth. Fuller was succeeded as prebendary by Davenant's nephews Robert and John Tounson. At the time of his appointment in 1633 John Tounson was in deacon's orders. Davenant presented Robert Tounson to the rectory of West Kington in 1633 and John to the vicarage of Bremhill in 1639. Another Tounson, William, presumably a relative, became prebendary of Minor Pars Altaris in 1622. Robert Davenant, another nephew, succeeded Robert Tounson at West

[1] His name is also rendered 'Townson' and 'Toulson'.
[2] *D.N.B.*
[3] Westminster Abbey Chapter Office, min. bk. f. 35 (6 Apr. 1624).
[4] See below.
[5] He held benefices at Fleet, Lincs., Leake, Notts., and Cottenham, Cambs.: *AC*.
[6] *D.N.B.*

Kington in 1633 and another, Edward Davenant, became rector of Poulshot and prebendary of Torleton in 1623, prebendary of Ilfracombe in 1624, archdeacon of Berkshire in 1631, prebendary of Chisenbury and Chute in 1632, and treasurer of Salisbury cathedral and prebendary of Calne in 1634. Davenant's most famous nephew was the younger Thomas Fuller, the Church historian, whom in 1634 Davenant appointed to the rectory of Broadwindsor (Dorset). Perhaps with justice Davenant has been described as 'a model uncle'.[1] Fuller's tutor, John Thorpe, also benefited from Davenant's patronage. Names occurring frequently in the subscription book are those of Davenant, Tounson, Thorpe, Hyde, Clerk, and Thornburgh, members of families clearly prominent in the diocese when Davenant was bishop. Davenant has also been described as 'a good type of the moderate Calvinist divine, but not equal either in extent of learning or in breadth of view to the divines of the Caroline era',[2] and, generally uncontroversial, he carried out Laud's policies faithfully. He was evidently moderate and fair-minded. In his episcopate many distinguished clergymen held benefices in the diocese, Puritans like Philip Hunton and Edward Fauconer, High Churchmen like Humphrey Henchman and John Earle who both became bishops of Salisbury, the scholar William Seaman, and the poet George Herbert. Subscriptions before Davenant were taken until 5 August 1640. He died eight months later on 20 April 1641. His failure to take subscriptions from the summer of 1640 suggests that his health had already begun to decline, although it is also possible that the attacks on the Church of England by the Puritans in Parliament in 1640 made him reluctant to enforce subscription to the articles in the last months of his life.

THE CLERGY

It appears from the subscription book that the main aims of the canons of 1604 were being carried out with regard to the qualifications of clergymen even if the strict letter of the canons was not always observed. The general level of education was high, at least so far as academic qualifications indicate it. Of the 813 clergymen who subscribed between 1620 and 1640[3] 383 were Masters of Arts and 303 Bachelors of Arts when they first subscribed. Among those holding higher degrees were 43 Bachelors of Divinity and 19 Doctors of Divinity, 12 Bachelors of Laws, 2 Bachelors of Civil Law, and 3 Doctors of Laws. Some 765 clergymen are known to have held degrees. There were nine, who, without degrees, described themselves as *litteratus*. Some of the remaining 39 subscribers held degrees which were not recorded at subscription. It seems likely that no more than 30, and perhaps fewer, of the clergy admitted in the period 1620–40 were not graduates. The Salisbury

[1] Ibid.
[2] Ibid.
[3] Including the schoolmaster (no. 372), who may have been in holy orders, and Richard Zsouche (no. 484), Regius Professor of Civil Law at Oxford, who, although a layman, held the prebend of Shipton with his chair.

diocese was therefore well on the way to achieving the standard of a wholly
graduate clergy aimed at in canon 34 of 1604. It was, however, still possible
to obtain preferment and even a general licence to preach without holding a
degree (e.g. no. 310). It is not possible to be sure what proportion of the
Salisbury clergy studied at each university because their colleges were usually
named in their subscriptions only by candidates for ordination. Other
subscribers usually stated their degree but not their college at subscription
and they cannot all be identified with certainty. Some of the clergy who
graduated at Oxford had their degrees incorporated at Cambridge and *vice
versa*. Of those whose university is known there was a clear, and in view of
the proximity of the university to the diocese, not surprising preponderance
of graduates from Oxford. Some Oxford dons seem to have sought ordination in the Salisbury diocese and some afterwards left the university and
became incumbents there. Although more remote, Cambridge also supplied
many of the diocese's clergy. One subscriber (no. 331) was a graduate of
Marischall's College, Aberdeen, another (no. 383) a graduate of Trinity
College, Dublin, and it is possible that others had graduated in Scotland or
at Dublin. Of those naming their college the greatest contingent came from
Magdalen College, Oxford. The subscriptions for ordination before Tounson
and Davenant show that in the period 1620–40 steady numbers of men were
coming forward for the ministry. Ordinations were frequent and, with very
few exceptions, the canon regarding the Ember seasons was faithfully
observed.

The leading patron of the parish clergy was the Crown with 64 presen-
tations and the deanery, like all cathedral deaneries, was a Crown appointment. Some 41 collations by the bishop are recorded, three by Tounson and
38 by Davenant, but that number is not high and a large proportion of the
collations was to prebends of the cathedral, few to parishes. His lack of
patronage clearly limited a bishop's ability to influence policy in the diocese
directly by appointment to livings. He could do so, however, by his appointments to prebends, and the senior positions of precentor, chancellor, and
treasurer with their attached benefices were in his gift. The bishop of
Salisbury was also patron of various livings outside his own diocese, especially in Dorset which had been severed from the diocese by Henry VIII as
part of the new see of Bristol. The landed gentry as a class had most control
of appointments in the Salisbury diocese. The earl of Pembroke was the
only nobleman with many livings at his disposal.

EDITORIAL METHOD

The material from the subscription book is printed below in the form of
translated and numbered abstracts. From each subscription is taken the
subscriber's name, the details, where stated, of his degree, college, and university, and the nature of his benefice, ordination, or licensing. Where an
identification is not in doubt the subscriber's degree, when not recorded in
the subscription book but known from another source, has been added in

square brackets. The dates which form the subheadings are those on which the subscriptions which follow them were made. They have been altered to accord with the modern reckoning of the beginning of the year. The 1,109 subscriptions in the book include many second or subsequent subscriptions by men already named. Each further subscription, beginning with its date, has been incorporated as a new paragraph after the record of the man's first subscription and not separately numbered. Cases of doubtful identification have been noted. The subscription book has been foliated but, because subscriptions are in chronological order, the folio numbers have not been printed. Forenames, usually in Latin in the original, have been translated. Where alternative forms of the forename or surname occur in the documents the first form has been followed and alternatives noted in round brackets. The spelling of forenames varied little and modern spellings have been adopted. There were, however, some remarkable differences in the fore-names a man might use. The clergy of the period sometimes found forenames a source of difficulty. The Puritans regarded saints' names as 'popish' and the Arminians regarded Old Testament names, and more so such names as 'Received' and 'Praise-God', as evidence of Puritanism. Only New Testament names were safe. Apparent changes of name, from 'Francis' to 'Henry' (no. 40) and from 'Paul' to 'Christopher' (no. 57), are not therefore surprising although there is no known evidence that the medieval and Roman Catholic custom of a candidate taking a new Christian name at confirmation or ordination survived in the Church of England. Surnames were rarely Latinized but where they were, for example in the forms 'Balaeus' and 'Hamandus', have been translated. Place-names, usually Latinized in the document, have been translated where to do so does not conflict with modern usage, and modern spellings, but not modern forms, have been adopted. Where the spelling in the manuscript differs significantly it has been given in round brackets after the modern spelling. Except for places in Wiltshire the county name has been added, in square brackets where it does not appear in the original.

The material in the subscription book has been added to from two other sources in the case of subscription on appointment to a benefice. Information is taken from the bishops' register of institutions[1] and in the abstracts follows '*Inst.*' and the relevant folio number of the register. The date of institution, omitted when it is the same as the date of subscription, the name of the patron of the living, and, where they are given, the name of the previous incumbent and the cause of the vacancy are printed. Since the main purpose of the register of institutions was to ensure the position of the new incumbent and to record that presentation had been made by the authorized patron, details of the previous incumbent and the cause of the vacancy were not always given. Cases where doubt about the validity of an institution seems to have arisen, often leading to a corroborative presentation by the Crown, are noted. The date on which an incumbent compounded for the first fruits and tenths and the names of his sureties are taken from the Exchequer

---

[1] In Salisbury Diocesan Registry.

registers of First Fruits and Tenths[1] and follow '*Comp.*' and the relevant document and folio numbers. Payment of first fruits and tenths to the Pope, introduced in England in the early 13th century, were the first year's whole profit and the tenth part of the annual profit of the benefice.[2] The amount to be paid, transferred to the Crown in the Reformation, was not changed after 1291 and by the early 17th century the taxes were not heavy burdens on the clergy. Instead of making a single payment incumbents, by compounding, paid by instalments, usually four at six-monthly intervals beginning six months after the composition was made. Compounding was optional and not all incumbents were named in the composition books. On the other hand, some compounded before they had been instituted (no. 181). Incumbents for whom there is no record of subscription but who are known from the registers of institutions and compositions are named at the date of their institution or compounding. The last recorded subscription before Bishop Davenant is dated 5 August 1640. Entries, abstracted below, continued in his institution book until 28 October 1640. Although compounding continued through the Civil War and Interregnum none made after 28 October 1640 has been abstracted.

At the end of each entry printed sources, in which biographical information about the subject of the entry may be found, are listed in abbreviated form in square brackets. The full titles of the works consulted and the abbreviations used are given in the list of abbreviations.[3]

[1] E 334/16–20.
[2] *Ecclesiastical Law*, ed. J. T. Edgerley, 468.
[3] See p. viii.

THE SUBSCRIPTION BOOK

13 July 1620
1 Thomas Lloyd, M.A., vicar of Wootton Bassett. *Inst.* (f. 1) on the death of Charles Primer; patron, Sir Charles Englefield. *Comp.* (334/16 f. 61) 27 Oct. 1620; sureties, John Edmonds, Thomas Alexander. [*AO, PR*]
2 John Still, M.A., rector of Tockenham. *Inst.* (f. 1) on a resignation; patron, the Crown. [*AO, FS, PR, WR*]

28 July 1620
3 John Bowle, S.T.P., chaplain to King James,[1] dean of Salisbury. *Inst.* (f. 1) on the translation of John Williams.[2] *Comp.* (334/16 f. 70) 1 Feb. 1621; sureties, Robert Coppin, Henry Brayton. [*ACO, DNB, FS*]

26 August 1620
4 Anthony Sarjeant, B.A., rector of Cricklade St. Mary. *Inst.* (f. 1) on the death of Ralph Butler; patron, Robert George. [*AO* (Sargeaunt), *PR*]
5 Marmaduke Lynne, LL.D., vicar general [of the diocese]. [*AC*]

23 September 1620
6 Roger Pinke, LL.B., rector of Old Stoke, Hants, ordained priest. [*AO, WR*]
7 John Gregson, B.A., ordained priest. [*AO, WR* p. 373, ? p. 337]
8 John Singleton, B.A., (Queen's, Oxf.), curate of Basildon, Berks., ordained priest.
 13 February 1637: vicar of Basildon. *Inst.* (f. 39) on a death; patron, the Crown. *Comp.* (334/18 f. 197) 16 Mar. 1637; sureties, Thomas Matthewe, Robert Giles. [*AO*]
9 Gabriel Reve (Reeve), M.A. (Winchester College and New, Oxf.), ordained deacon. [*AO*]
10 John Lewis, B.A. (Magdalen, Oxf.), curate of Great Cheverell, ordained deacon. [*AO*]
11 Edward Bankes, B.A. (Magdalen, Oxf.), ordained deacon.
 24 December 1620: ordained priest. [*ACO*]
12 Knightley Wallis, B.A. (Hart Hall, Oxf.), ordained deacon. [*AO*]
13 Thomas Browne, B.A. (Brasenose, Oxf.), curate of Harbridge, Hants, ordained deacon. [*AO, CR* p. 81]
14 Thomas Wilcox, B.A. (St. Mary Hall, Oxf.), curate of Semington [Steeple Ashton parish], ordained deacon. [*AO*]
15 Thomas Northey, M.A., vicar of Broad Hinton. *Inst.* (f. 1) on the death of Thomas Crapon; patron, St. Nicholas Hospital, Salisbury. *Comp.* (334/16 f. 59) 4 Oct. 1620; sureties, William Northey, Christopher Stronge.
 5 October 1620: licensed to preach.

---

[1] A royal chaplaincy, carrying the duty of preaching before the sovereign, was usually given to a clergyman of unquestionable orthodoxy rising to prominence in the Church.
[2] To the deanery of Westminster. Williams was later archbishop of York: *D.N.B.*

16 September 1620: vicar of Potterne. *Inst.* (f. 26) on the death of Nicholas Strangridge; patron, John Gent. *Comp.* (334/17 f. 203) 21 Nov. 1629; sureties, Edward Northey, Anthony Neate. [*AO*, *PR*]

16 James Chadwick, M.A. (Brasenose, Oxf.), curate of Aldbourne, ordained priest.

    6 October 1629: licensed to preach. [*AO*, *WR*]

17 Edward Holland, B.A. (Corpus Christi, Oxf.), ordained deacon.

    16 June 1622: ordained priest. [*AO*]

29 September 1620

18 Christopher Wren, S.T.B., rector of Fonthill Bishop. *Inst.* (f. 1) on the death of Dominicke Clerk; patron, Lancelot, bishop of Winchester. *Comp.* (334/16 f. 61) 25 Oct. 1620; sureties, Francis Wren, Wolstan Randall.

    18 June 1623: rector of Bishop's Knoyle. *Inst.* (f. 17) on the resignation of Ralph Barlow; patron, Lancelot, bishop of Winchester. *Comp.* (334/16 f. 152) 7 July 1623; sureties, Francis Wren, Wolstan Randall. [*AO*, *DNB* (s.v. Sir Christopher Wren), *PR*, *WR*]

4 October 1620

19 William Twiss (Twisse), S.T.D., rector of Newbury, Berks. *Inst.* (f. 1) on the resignation of Nathaniel Giles; patron, Charles Stuart, prince of Wales. *Comp.* (334/16 f. 62) 2 Nov. 1620; sureties, John Pocock, Robert Hamond. [*AO*, *DNB*]

20 John Badcock, M.A. (Magdalen, Oxf.), licensed to preach at Market Lavington. [*AO*]

21 Robert Bright, B.A. (Broadgates Hall, Oxf.), curate of Kemble. [*AO*]

5 October 1620

22 Robert Rogers, M.A., rector of Heddington, licensed to preach. [? *AO*] [*and see* no. 15]

6 October 1620

23 John Lynch, M.A., vicar of Aldbourne, licensed to preach. [*ACO*, *FS*, *WR* p. 221]

24 John Sneele, M.A., rector of Shorncote, licensed to preach. [*ACO* (Snell)]

25 Richard Stubbs, B.A., vicar of Hannington, licensed to preach. [*AO*] [*and see* no. 16]

10 October 1620

26 John Squier, B.A., curate of Kintbury, Berks., licensed to preach.

    23 February 1627: vicar of Brimpton, Berks. *Inst.* (f. 23) on the death of Lancelot Hodson; patron, William Wollascot. [*AO*]

27 Simon Wilkes, M.A., licensed to preach in the diocese. [*AO*]

28 Richard Gardiner (Gardyner), M.A., licensed to preach in the diocese.

    7 July 1627: vicar of East Garston, Berks. *Inst.* (f. 23) 17 July 1627 on the death of Hugh Jones; patron, the dean and chapter of Christ Church, Oxford. *Comp.* (334/17 f. 127) 19 July 1627; sureties, James Croft, William Moon. [*ACO*, *DNB*]

12 October 1620
29 Theophilus Taylor, M.A., vicar of St. Lawrence's, Reading, Berks., licensed to preach in the diocese. [*AC*]
30 Charles Winne, M.A., licensed to preach in the diocese. [*AO*]
31 Peter Fawkner, M.A., licensed to preach in the diocese. [*AO*]
32 Anthony White, M.A., licensed to preach in the diocese. [*ACO*]
33 Thomas Singleton, M.A., licensed to preach in the diocese.[1] [*AO*]

16 October 1620
34 Thomas Mason, S.T.B., rector of Manningford Abbots, licensed to preach. *Inst.* (f. 1) on the death of Thomas Bromley; patron, Edward Seymour, earl of Hertford. *Comp.* (334/16 f. 61) 25 Oct. 1620; sureties, John Johnson, John Anman.
  25 August 1624: prebendary of Alton Australis; patron, the bishop. *Comp.* (334/17 f. 28) 9 Nov. 1624; sureties, John Anman, John Johnson. [*AO, DNB, FS, PR, WR*]

18 October 1620
35 Ellis Tise, rector of Biddestone St. Peter. *Inst.* (f. 1) on a death; patron, the Crown.
  25 June 1638: licensed to preach in the diocese. [*PR*]

24 November 1620
36 John (Hugh) Brian (Bryan), M.A., rector of Wingfield, licensed to preach. *Inst.* (f. 2) on the death of Robert Comyn; patron, Henry Sherfield. [*AO, PR*]

28 November 1620
37 Edward Wilson, [B.D.,] vicar of Wantage, Berks. No subscription or institution.[2] *Comp.* (334/16 f. 65); sureties, William Moore, John Wilson. [*AO*]

29 November 1620
38 Walter Curle, S.T.D., rector of Fugglestone and Bemerton.[3] *Inst.* (f. 2) on the death of William Lewis; patron, John Bowles. *Comp.* (334/16 f. 70) 2 Feb. 1621; sureties, Edward Curle, John Manningham. [*ACO, DNB, FS, PR, WR* p. 17]
39 Francis South, rector of Ebbesborne Wake. No subscription or institution.[4] *Comp.* (334/16 f. 65); sureties, Ellis Swaine, John South. [*AC*]

6 December 1620
40 Francis (Henry) Sayer (Sawyer), M.A., rector of Yattendon, Berks. *Inst.* (f. 2) on the resignation of Samuel Watkins; patron, Francis Norreys. *Comp.* (334/16 f. 69) 3 Jan. 1621; sureties, John Sayer, Richard Jackson.

---

[1] The subscription is dated 11 Oct. Since it comes in a group of similar subscriptions dated 12 Oct. that date appears to have been written in error.
[2] Wantage was a peculiar of the dean and canons of Windsor: *V.C.H. Berks.* iv. 392.
[3] Bemerton was a chapelry of Fugglestone: *V.C.H. Wilts.* vi. 37.
[4] The rectory was attached to the office of sub-chanter of Salisbury cathedral: Hoare, *Mod. Wilts.* Chalke, 164–5.

31 January 1626: rector of Milton, Berks., licensed to preach. *Inst.* (f. 21) on the death of Edmund Colepepper; patron, Richard Sawyer. *Comp.* (334/17 f. 73) 9 Feb. 1626; sureties, Edward Sayer, John Ruffin. [*AO*]

24 December 1620

41 Richard Atkinson, B.A. (Magdalen, Oxf.), ordained deacon. [*AO*]

42 John Palmer, B.A. (Oriel, Oxf.), ordained deacon.

10 June 1623: vicar of Upavon. *Inst.* (f. 17) on a resignation; patron, the Crown. [*AO*]

43 Anthony South, [B.A.] (St. Edmund Hall, Oxf.), ordained deacon. [*AO*] [*and see no.* 11]

13 January 1621

44 Walter Ralegh (Raleigh), M.A., rector of St. Mary's, Wilton, and vicar of Bulbridge.[1] *Inst.* (f. 2); patron, William, earl of Pembroke.

14 December 1632: rector of Wroughton (Elingdon). *Inst.* (f. 30) on the death of Thomas Bysse; patron, the Crown. *Comp.* (334/18 f. 89) 4 June 1633; sureties, Richard Franklin, William Morse. [*AO, DNB, PR, WR*]

8 January 1621[2]

45 William Prynne (Prin),[3] S.T.B., rector of Easthampstead, Berks. *Inst.* (f. 2) 8 Feb. 1621; patrons, Richard Wightwicke and William Hyford. [*AO*]

5 March 1621

46 Matthew Nicholas, LL.B. (New, Oxf.), ordained deacon, rector of West Dean. *Inst.* (f. 2) on the death of William Tooker; patron, George Evelyn. *Comp.* (334/16 f. 74) 6 Mar. 1621; sureties, John Nicholas, Edward Nicholas.

24 February 1628: prebendary of Gillingham Minor. *Inst.* (f. 24) on the death of John Odell ; patron, the bishop.

4 December 1630: master of St. Nicholas Hospital, Salisbury. *Inst.* (f. 28) on the death of Geoffrey Bigg; patron, John Nicholas. [*AO, DNB, FS, PR, WR*]

7 March 1621

47 Henry Burford, M.A. (St. John's, Oxf.), vicar of Clyffe Pypard. *Inst.* (f. 2); patron, the Crown.

2 October 1622: licensed to preach in the diocese. [*AO* (Bedford), *PR*]

8 March 1621

48 Samuel Fell, S.T.P., rector of Longworth, Berks. *Inst.* (f. 2) on the resignation of George Warburton; patron, Sir Henry Marten. *Comp.* (334/16 f. 79) 26 Apr. 1621; sureties, Simon Harborne, William Pembrooke.

18 January 1626: rector of Sunningwell, Berks. *Inst.* (f. 21) on a death; patron, the Crown. *Comp.* (334/17 f. 77) 1 Mar. 1626; sureties, Simon Harborne, Marmaduke Claver. [*AO, DNB, WR*]

---

[1] St. Peter's, Bulbridge, was united with St. Mary's, Wilton, in 1593: *V.C.H. Wilts.* vi. 31.
[2] This entry stands out of chronological sequence in the original for no apparent reason.
[3] Cf. no. 156 and n.

12 March 1621
49 Richard Chandler, M.A. (Hart Hall, Oxf.), rector of St. Mary's, Wilton. *Inst.* (f. 2); patron, William, earl of Pembroke. *Comp.* (334/16 f. 75) 14 Mar. 1621; sureties, Robert Chandler, Thomas Willett.
  29 April 1634: prebendary of Lyme and Halstock. No subscription or institution.[1] *Comp.* (334/18 f. 114) 29 Apr. 1634; sureties, Robert Chandler, William Pittisland. [*AO, FS, PR, WR*]

14 March 1621
50 William Tounson, M.A., prebendary of Minor Pars Altaris.
  25 November 1622: prebendary of Minor Pars Altaris.[2] *Inst.* (f. 16) 24 Nov. 1622; patron, the bishop. *Comp.* (334/16 f. 142) 9 Apr. 1623; sureties, William Ireland, John Stodgell. [*AC, FS*]

13 May 1621
51 Nathaniel Cannon, S.T.B., vicar of Shottesbrook, Berks. *Inst.* (f. 2) 3 May on the death of Thomas Howe; patron, Lewis James. [*AO*]

1 October 1621[3]
52 William Noble, [M.A.,] rector of Luckington. No subscription or institution. *Comp.* (334/16 f. 93); sureties, Richard Noble, Edmund Slater. [*AO*]

8 October 1621
53 Thomas Bayly, [B.D.,] rector of Manningford Bruce. No subscription or institution. *Comp.* (334/16 f. 93); sureties, Thomas Browne, John Nicholls. [*AO* (Baylie), *DNB*]

9 October 1621
54 John Coothe, [M.A.,] prebendary of Grimstone and Yetminster. No subscription or institution. *Comp.* (334/16 f. 93); sureties, George Poldon, Gilbert Harrison. [*AO*]

12 October 1621
55 John Seller, [M.A.,] rector of Didcot, Berks. No subscription or institution. *Comp.* (334/16 f. 94); sureties, Laurence Seller, Thomas Bernard. [*AO*]

17 November 1621
56 Thomas Pelling, [B.A.,] rector of Trowbridge. No subscription or institution.[4] *Comp.* (334/16 f. 99); sureties, Edward Grove, Henry Reynolds. [*AO, WR*]

18 November 1621
57 Paul (Christopher) Hood, S.T.B., rector of Broughton Gifford. *Inst.* (f. 14)

---

[1] For no obvious reason. The cathedral prebends were in the bishop's gift.
[2] Tounson was appointed in Nov. 1622: *FS.* It is possible that an attempt to find for him a better endowed prebend than that of Minor Pars Altaris failed after the death in May 1622 of Bishop Tounson, possibly his father.
[3] The lack of subscriptions June–Oct. 1621 for livings under the bishop's ordinary jurisdiction was due to the vacancy of the see 15 June – 18 Nov.
[4] Trowbridge was a peculiar: Sar. Dioc. R.O., *Guide*, 106.

on a death; patron, the Crown. *Comp.* (334/16 f. 99) 22 Nov. 1621; sureties, George Karver, Abell Alleyn. [*ACO, PR, WR* p. 280]
58 Edward Boughen, M.A., vicar of Bray, Berks. *Inst.* (f. 14); patron, John, bishop of Oxford. *Comp.* (334/16 f. 101) 8 Dec. 1621; sureties, John Gwalter, Richard Gwalter. [*AO, DNB, WR* p. 212]

28 November 1621
59 William Stumpe, [B.A.,] rector of Yatton Keynell. No subscription or institution.[1]   *Comp.* (334/16 f. 100); sureties, Peter Birde, Robert Smith. [*ACO*]

15 February 1622
60 Nathan (Nathaniel) Noyes, B.A., rector of Cholderton. *Inst.* (f. 14) 5 Feb. 1622 on the resignation of William Noyes; patron, Edward, Lord Zouche St. Maur. *Comp.* (334/16 f. 110) 23 Mar. 1622; sureties, Thomas Guye, Walter Braggs. [*AO, Conc. Test., PR*]
61 John Smith *alias* Howell, M.A., vicar of Broad Chalke, Bower Chalke, and Alvediston.[2] *Inst.* (f. 14) on the death of John Archer; patron, King's College, Cambridge. *Comp.* (334/16 f. 111) 6 April 1622 (Broad Chalke and Bower Chalke); sureties, Robert Howell *alias* Smith, Eleazar Howell *alias* Smith. *Comp.* (334/16 f. 111) 30 Apr. 1622 (Alvediston); sureties, Robert Howell *alias* Smith, Eleazar Howell *alias* Smith. [*AC, PR*]

20 February 1622
62 Robert Bonython (Bonithon), M.A., rector of Woolhampton, Berks., and vicar of Thatcham, Berks. *Inst.* (f. 14) 31 May 1622 on the deprivation of Ralph Fawkoner; patron, Henry Winchcombe. *Comp.* (334/16 f. 118) 7 June 1622; sureties, Thomas Bonython, Henry Cotham. [*AO*]

15 June 1622
63 Jerome Newman, [M.A.,] ordained deacon. [*AO*]
64 Robert Ingall, M.A. (Queen's, Oxf.), ordained priest. [*AO*]
65 John Wolston, B.A. (Gloucester Hall, Oxf.), curate of Shottesbrook, (Shasbrook), Berks., ordained deacon.
   21 December 1622: curate of Remenham, Berks., ordained priest. [*AO*]
66 Matthew Bennett, B.A., curate of Allington, ordained priest. [*AO, WR* p. 42]
67 John Carpenter, [B.A.,] ordained priest. [*AO*]
68 Edward Bridges, M.A., curate of Dauntsey, ordained priest.
   2 October 1622: licensed to preach in the diocese.
   5 March 1627: vicar of Seagry. *Inst.* (f. 23) 14 Mar. 1627 on the death of William Jones; patron, Henry, earl of Danby.
   9 February 1628: rector of Bremilham. *Inst.* (f. 24) on the death of Richard Fayne; patron, Henry, earl of Danby. [*AO*]

[1] For no obvious reason.
[2] Three neighbouring but separate parishes in the gift of King's Coll., Camb.

16 June 1622
69 Thomas Braffield.[1]
[*and see* no. 17]

21 June 1622
70 Francis Slade, [M.A.,] vicar of Wantage, Berks. No subscription or institution.[2] *Comp.* (334/16 f. 119); sureties, Thomas Stevins, Edward Scoles. [*AO*]

27 June 1622
71 Francis White, M.A., vicar of Ashbury, Berks. *Inst.* (f. 15) on the death of Roger Webster; patron, Sir Henry Marten. *Comp.* (334/16 f. 120) 3 July 1622; sureties, Edward White, Richard Higgs. [*AO*]
72 William Moore (More), M.A., vicar of Compton, Berks. *Inst.* (f. 15) on the resignation of Joseph Nixon; patron, Sir Henry Marten. *Comp.* (334/16 f. 123) 27 July 1622; sureties, Francis Foxe, Augustine Springhall.

1 February 1630: vicar of Hampstead Norris, Berks. *Inst.* (f. 26) on the death of Richard Whitwick; patron, James Vanloor. [? *ACO*]

1 July 1622
73 Richard Heal.[3]

10 July 1622
74 Hugh Goodman, M.A., vicar of Stanford-in-the-Vale, Berks. *Inst.* (f. 15) on the death of George Davies; patrons, the dean and chapter of Westminster. *Comp.* (334/16 f. 123) 24 July 1622; sureties, Thomas Goodman, Thomas Parker.

26 July 1622
75 John Weston, B.A., vicar of Cholsey, Berks. *Inst.* (f. 15) on a cession; patron, the Crown. *Comp.* (334/16 f. 124) 22 Aug. 1622; sureties, Thomas Buckner, Rowland Holt. [*AO*, *WR* p. 62]
76 John Forsith, B.A., rector of Sedgehill.[4] *Inst.* (f. 15); patron, the Crown. [*PR*]

22 August 1622
77 John Clare, S.T.B., rector of Yattendon, Berks. *Inst.* (f. 15); patron, the Crown. [*AO*]

3 September 1622
78 John King, M.A., rector of Remenham, Berks. *Inst.* (f. 15) on the death of John Newman; patron, Sir Henry Marten. *Comp.* (334/16 f. 127) 1 Oct. 1622; sureties, Henry King, William Stanfield. [*AO* (Kinge), *DNB*]

---

[1] MS. damaged.
[2] See no. 37 and n. Slade subscribed before the dean 1 Mar. 1622.
[3] MS. damaged.
[4] Sedgehill later became a chapelry of Berwick St. Leonard: *Returns to Visitation Queries 1783*, ed. Mary Ransome (W.R.S. xxvii), p. 188.

6 September 1622. [1]
79 Walter Waller, M.A., vicar of Broad Chalke with Bower Chalke and Alvediston. [2] *Inst.* (f. 15) on the resignation of John Smith; patron, King's College, Cambridge. *Comp.* (334/16 f. 126) 16 Sept. 1622; sureties, William Boswell, Nathaniel Tomkins. [*AC, PR*]

13 September 1622
80 Edward Thornburgh, M.A., prebendary of Preston. *Inst.* (f. 15) on the death of Richard Johnson; patron, the bishop. [*AO, FS, WR*]

18 September 1622
81 Daniel Berry (Bury), M.A., rector of Wasing, Berks. *Inst.* (f. 15) on a death; patron, the Crown. [*AO, WR* p. 109]

21 September 1622
82 Richard Foot (Foote), M.A. (Exeter, Oxf.), ordained deacon.
   6 March 1624: vicar of Tilshead. *Inst.* (f. 19) on a resignation; patron, the Crown.
   19 September 1624: ordained priest. [*AO, WR*]
83 John Smith, M.A. (St. Mary Hall, Oxf.), ordained deacon.
   21 September 1623: ordained priest. [*AO*]
84 Thomas Watson, M.A. (Oriel, Oxf.), curate of Ludgershall, ordained deacon.
   21 December 1622: curate of Langley [Eling parish], Hants, ordained priest. [*AO*]
85 John Smith, B.A. (Oriel, Oxf.), curate of St. Lawrence's, Reading, Berks., ordained priest. [*AO*]
86 John Barker, B.A. (Clare, Camb.), curate of Stourpaine, Dors., ordained deacon.
   21 December 1623: ordained priest.
   18 May 1636: vicar of Speen, Berks. *Inst.* (f. 37) on the death of Richard Watt; patron, the bishop. [*AC*]
87 William Hinwood, B.A. (Oriel, Oxf.), ordained deacon.
   19 September 1624: curate of Greenham, Berks., ordained priest. [*AO*]
88 Philip Goddard, B.A. (St. Mary Hall, Oxf.), ordained deacon. [*AO*]
89 Richard Humphreys, B.A. (St. Edmund Hall, Oxf.), ordained deacon.
   8 June 1623: curate of Sedgehill, ordained priest. [*AO*]

2 October 1622
90 Moses Clayton, B.A., licensed to preach in the diocese. [*AO*]
91 Robert Merick, M.A., licensed to preach in the diocese. [*AO*]
[*and see* nos. 47, 68]

3 October 1622
92 Oliver Bunsell, B.A., licensed to preach in the diocese.
93 Thomas Smarte, licensed to preach in the diocese.

---

[1] The subscription is dated 6 Aug. but its position in the MS. and the date of Waller's institution suggest that that was a mistake for 6 Sept.
[2] See no. 61 and n.

17 June 1623: vicar of Eisey. *Inst.* (f. 17) on the death of Humphrey Smith; patron, Edward Sheldon. *Comp.* (334/16 f. 154) 8 Aug. 1623; sureties, John Cox, Anthony Portlocke. [*AC* (Smart)][1]

94 John Elliot, B.A., licensed to preach in the diocese. [? *AC*]

95 Robert Freak, B.A., licensed to preach in the diocese. [*AO*]

4 October 1622

96 Robert Whitefield, M.A., licensed to preach in the diocese. [*AO*, *Conc. Test.*]

97 Thomas Osborne, M.A., licensed to preach in the diocese. [? *ACO*]

5 October 1622

98 Thomas Twisse, M.A., licensed to preach in the diocese. [*AO*]

99 John Stone, M.A., licensed to preach in the diocese. 22 May 1635: rector of St. Nicholas's, Abingdon, Berks. *Inst.* (f. 36) on the resignation of William Webber; patron, the Crown. *Comp.* (334/18 f. 153) June 1635;[2] sureties, Charles Tooker, James Heron. [*AO*]

100 John Gumbledon, B.A., licensed to preach in the diocese. [*AO*]

101 John Place, B.A., licensed to preach in the diocese. 19 January 1632: vicar of Denchworth, Berks. *Inst.* (f. 29) on a death; patrons, William Cockayne, Matthew Cradocke, James Price. 13 April 1636: vicar of Ardington, Berks. *Inst.* (f. 37) on the resignation of Michael Berwicke; patron, the dean and chapter of Christ Church, Oxford. [*AO*]

7 October 1622

102 Thomas Middleton, M.A., rector of Brightwalton, Berks., licensed to preach in the diocese. *Inst.* on the resignation of Thomas Morland; patrons, Richard Knight, Martin Morland. *Comp.* (334/16 f. 128) 21 Oct. 1622; sureties, Robert Brigge, John Shipton. [*AO*]

21 October 1622

103 Polydore Evans, B.A., licensed to preach in the diocese. [*AO*, *WR* p. 312]

30 October 1622

104 Thomas Payne, B.A., vicar of Longbridge Deverill and Monkton Deverill.[3] *Inst.* (f. 16) on the resignation of William Gay; patron, Sir Thomas Thynne. *Comp.* (334/16 f. 147) 29 May 1623; sureties, William Gatehouse, William Cole. [*AO*, *PR*, *WR*]

15 November 1622

105 John Bradford, [M.A.,] vicar of Blewbury, Berks. No subscription or institution.[4] *Comp.* (334/16 f. 131); sureties, Thomas Goodman, Thomas Packe. [*AO*]

---

[1] Probably the Thomas Smarte who matriculated 1611 but apparently did not graduate.
[2] Day of the month not given.
[3] Adjacent but separate livings in the gift of Sir Thomas Thynne.
[4] Blewbury was a peculiar of the dean of Salisbury. Bradford subscribed before the dean 28 Sept. 1622.

25 November 1622
[*see* no. 50]

12 December 1622
106 Thomas Buckley, S.T.B., vicar of Damerham. *Inst.* (f. 16) on the death of John Humphrey; patron, William, earl of Salisbury. *Comp.* (334/16 f. 133) 3 Dec. 1622; sureties, Samuel Stillingfleet, Christopher Highley. [*AC, PR*]

14 December 1622
107 Edward Simpsion, rector of Ditteridge. *Inst.* (f. 16) on the death of Philip Pellinger; patron, Anthony Bolwell. [? *AC* (Simson), *PR*]

19 December 1622
108 Frederick Vaughan, [M.A.] (Queen's, Oxf.), ordained priest. [*AO, WR* pp. 137–8]

21 December 1622
109 Robert Ritch, B.A. (Balliol, Oxf.), curate of Brinkworth, ordained priest. [*AO*, ? *WR* p. 256]

19 December 1622[1]
110 James Weaver (Christ Church, Oxf.), ordained priest.[2]

21 December 1622
111 Henry Munden, B.A. (Gonville and Caius, Camb.), curate of Long Crichel, Dors., ordained deacon. [*AC*]
112 Richard Broadhead, B.A. (Christ Church, Oxf.), curate of Charlton, ordained deacon.
    21 December 1623: ordained priest. [*AO*]
113 John Lee, B.A. (All Souls', Oxf.), curate of Wylye, ordained priest.
    29 April 1624: treasurer of Salisbury cathedral, prebendary of Calne.[3] *Inst.* (f. 19) on the death of Thomas White; patron, the bishop. *Comp.* (334/17 f. 13) 11 May 1624; sureties, John Mariot, Caleb Stephens.
    24 February 1630: rector of Little Langford. *Inst.* (f. 27) on the death of John Antram; patron, William, earl of Pembroke. *Comp.* (334/18 f. 210) 5 Feb. 1630; sureties, Jepson Jewell, John Marriott. [*AO, FS*]
114 Edward Hancock, B.A. (Oriel, Oxf.), curate of Winterslow, ordained deacon.
    8 June 1623: ordained priest. [*AO*]
115 Richard Turner, M.A. (Broadgates Hall, Oxf.), curate of . . . ,[4] Dors., ordained priest.[5]
116 William Ringe,[6] B.A. (St. Alban Hall, Oxf.), curate of Semington [Steeple Ashton parish], ordained deacon.

---

1 It is not clear why this subscription is out of the chronological sequence. It is possible that Weaver swore his oaths 19 Dec. and recorded his subscription 21 Dec., but equally possible that he entered the wrong date when subscribing on 21 Dec.
2 There is no entry for Weaver in *AO*.
3 The prebend was attached to the treasurership: *FS*, ii. 234.
4 MS. damaged.
5 *AO* records several Richard Turners but none graduating at Broadgates.
6 Cf. no 164 and n.

21 December 1623: ordained priest. [*AO*]
117 William Lipyeatt, B.A. (St. Edmund Hall, Oxf.), curate of Maiden Bradley, ordained deacon.
19 December 1624: ordained priest. [*AO*]
118 Francis Twigden, B.A. (Queen's, Oxf.), curate of Little Cheverell, ordained deacon. [*AO*]
119 Thomas Yarde, M.A. (Broadgates Hall, Oxf.), ordained deacon.
21 December 1623: ordained priest.
16 October 1624: licensed to preach in the diocese.
8 December 1635: rector of Berwick St. John. *Inst.* (f. 37) 18 Dec. 1635 on the resignation of Robert Pinckney; patron, Thomas Wallis. *Comp.* (334/18 f. 171) 8 Mar. 1636; sureties, John Butler, Robert Grove. [*AO*]
120 William Smith, M.A. (St. Edmund Hall, Oxf.), ordained deacon.
23 July 1623: rector of Castle Eaton. *Inst.* (f. 18) on the death of Humphrey Smith; patron, Sir John Hungerford. *Comp.* (334/16 f. 154) 21 Aug. 1623; sureties, Francis Parker, John Brooker.
6 October 1623: rector of Castle Eaton. *Inst.* (f. 18); patron, the Crown.[1] [*AO*]
121 William Noyes, M.A. (Magdalen, Oxf.), ordained deacon. [*AO*]
122 Lancelot Moorhouse, B.A. (Jesus, Camb.), curate of Broad Chalke, ordained priest.
28 March 1638: rector of Pertwood. *Inst.* (f. 43) on the cession of Richard Mervyn; patron, George Mervyn. [*AC*]
123 Hugh Williams, M.A. (St. Edmund Hall, Oxf.), curate of Pewsey, ordained priest. [*AO*]
[*and see* nos. 65, 84]

24 December 1622
124 Humphrey Wall, M.A., vicar of Stapleford. *Inst.* (f. 16) on the resignation of Percy Medlam; patron, the dean and chapter of Windsor. [*AO* (Walls), *PR*]

20 January 1623
125 Humphrey Henchman,[2] M.A., Fellow of Clare, Camb., precentor of Salisbury cathedral, licensed to preach. *Inst.* (f. 16) as precentor and rector of Westbury[3] on the death of Henry Cotton; patron, the bishop.
26 February 1623: prebendary of Yatesbury. *Inst.* (f. 17) on the resignation of Hugh Gough; patron, the bishop. *Comp.* (334/16 f. 142) 9 Apr. 1623 as precentor, prebendary of Yatesbury, and prebendary of Highworth;[4] sureties, William Ireland, John Stogdell.
27 February 1629: prebendary of Grantham Australis. *Inst.* (f. 25) on the death of William Beekesdale; patron, the bishop.
5 January 1639: prebendary of Teinton and Yalmeton. *Inst.* (f. 45) on

[1] The presentation by the Crown was corroborative.
[2] Bishop of Salisbury 1660–3.
[3] The rectory was attached to the office of precentor: *V.C.H. Wilts.* viii. 176.
[4] Cf. no. 126 and n.

the death of Samuel Proctor; patron, the bishop.

10 July 1640: commissary or vicar general [of the diocese]. [*AC, DNB, FS*]

30 January 1623

126 Thomas Fuller, S.T.B., rector of Aldwincle, Northants., prebendary of Highworth.[1] *Inst.* (f. 16) on the death of Henry Cotton; patron, the bishop.

18 June 1631: prebendary of Netherbury in Ecclesia. *Inst.* (f. 28) on the death of John Rawlinson; patron, the bishop. [*AC, DNB, PR, WR* pp. 47–8]

127 Edward Davenant, M.A., Fellow of Queens', Camb., rector of Poulshot. *Inst.* (f. 16) on the death of Henry Cotton; patron, the bishop.

16 August 1623: prebendary of Torleton. *Inst.* (f. 18) on the death of William Harward; patron, the bishop.

23 February 1624: prebendary of Ilfracombe. *Inst.* (f. 19) on the death of William Caulborn; patron, the bishop.

26 January 1631: archdeacon of Berkshire, rector of North Moreton, Berks.[2] *Inst.* (f. 28) 16 Jan. 1631 on the death of Lionel Sharpe; patron, the bishop. *Comp.* (334/18 f. 8) 24 Mar. 1631; sureties, William Ireland, John Greene.

14 June 1632: prebendary of Chute and Chisenbury. *Inst.* (f. 30) on the death of John Thorpe; patron, the bishop. *Comp.* (334/18 f. 64) 21 Oct. 1632; sureties, John Butler, John Bishop.

19 November 1634: treasurer of Salisbury cathedral and prebendary of Calne.[3] *Inst.* (f. 33) on the death of John Lee, patron, the bishop. *Comp.* (334/18 f. 136) 26 Nov. 1634; sureties, Henry Clinket, William Tiffin. [*AC, FS, PR, WR*]

7 February 1623

128 Peter Waterman, M.A., rector of Sopworth. *Inst.* (f. 16) on a resignation; patron, the Crown. *Comp.* (334/16 f. 162) 28 Nov. 1623; sureties, Robert Sherfield, Ambrose Prewer.

28 January 1630: rector of Wootton Rivers. *Inst.* (f. 26) on the death of John Cooley; patron, Roger Sherfield. *Comp.* (334/18 f. 218) 12 May 1630; sureties, Henry Sherfield, Edward Sherfield. [*AO, PR, WR*]

23 February 1623

129 Peter Thatcher, M.A., rector of St. Edmund's, Salisbury. *Inst.* (f. 16) on the resignation of Hugh Williams; patron, the bishop. [*AO, PR*]

26 February 1623

[*see* no. 125]

11 March 1623

130 John Hyll (Hill), M.A., vicar of Ashton Keynes. *Inst.* (f. 17) on the death

---

[1] Fuller was Bishop Davenant's brother-in-law: *D.N.B.* Highworth had possibly been intended for Henchman (no. 125), who had Yatesbury instead, but was given to Fuller. The record of Henchman, not Fuller, compounding for Highworth presumably arises from a mistake.

[2] The rectory was appropriated to the archdeaconry between 1535 and the reign of Charles I: *V.C.H. Berks.* iii. 498.

[3] See no. 113 n.

of Thomas Awbrey; patron, Jonas Hill. *Comp.* (334/16 f. 142) 9 Apr. 1623; sureties, Edward Orwell, John Walsall. [? *ACO, PR*]

19 March 1623
131 John Hayes, M.A., vicar of Overton. *Inst.* (f. 17) 29 Mar. 1623 on the death of Thomas Clifford; patron, William, earl of Pembroke. *Comp.* (334/16 f. 144) 25 Apr. 1623; sureties, William Feltham, Christopher Gray. [*AO, PR*]

2 April 1623
132 John Potter, M.A., licensed to preach at West Dean and in the diocese.
  11 October 1638: rector of Binfield, Berks. *Inst.* (f. 44) on a cession; patron, the Crown. *Comp.* (334/18 f. 247) 5 Nov. 1638; sureties, John Higgens, Thomas Nicholls. [*AO*]

12 April 1623
133 John South, B.C.L., rector of Allington. *Inst.* (f. 17) on the death of Nicholas Fuller; patron, Sir Henry Wallop. *Comp.* (334/16 f. 148) 10 June 1623; sureties, Richard South, Lambert Osbolton. [*AO, PR, WR* p. 163]

28 April 1623
134 Thomas Clark, S.T.P., prebendary of Uffculme. *Inst.* (f. 17) on the death of Nicholas Fuller; patron, the bishop. *Comp.* (334/16 f. 147) 29 May 1623; sureties, John Orlibeare, William Spurway.
  27 July 1624: rector of Manningford Abbots. *Inst.* (f. 19) on the resignation of Thomas Mason; patron, Sir Francis Seymour. *Comp.* (334/17 f. 22) 28 Aug. 1624; sureties, William Clarke, Edward Meredithe. [*AO, PR, WR*]
135 Renewed (Renovatus) Jessop, B.A., licensed to preach at St. Mary's and St. John's, Devizes. [*AO*]

23 May 1623
136 Thomas Bisse, [M.A.,] vicar of Wroughton (Elingdon). No subscription or institution.[1] *Comp.* (334/16 f. 147); sureties, Jeremy Ferrar, Samuel Nayle. [*AO, PR*]

5 June 1623
137 Laurence Barlow, M.A., licensed to preach at Nettleton and in the diocese.
  21 March 1629: rector of Nettleton. *Inst.* (f. 25) on the death of Edward Hutchins; patrons, Francis Shearce and William Hutchins. *Comp.* (334/17 f. 185) 9 May 1629; sureties, John Thorner, Otwell Barlow. [*AO*]

8 June 1623
138 Henry Colepepper, M.A., vicar of Enford. *Inst.* (f. 17) on the death of Thomas Floyd; patrons, Henry Crispe and John Thorpe. *Comp.* (334/16 f. 151) 4 July 1623; sureties, Robert Kefax, Peter Johnson. [*AO* (Culpepper), *Conc. Test., PR*]
139 Thomas Payne, B.A., curate of Tincleton, Dors., ordained priest. [*AO*]

[1] For no obvious reason. Wroughton was under the bishop's regular jurisdiction.

140 William Walton, B.A., curate of Wynford Eagle, Dors., ordained priest. [*AC*]

141 William Rous, B.A., curate of Stoke Gaylard [Lydlinch parish], Dors., ordained deacon. [*AO*]

142 Robert Pleydell, B.A., curate of Blunsdon St. Andrew, ordained deacon. [*AO*]

143 Robert Odell, M.A., curate of Winterborne Houghton (Howton), Dors., ordained deacon. [*AO*]

144 John Bushell, B.A., curate of Stratford sub Castle, ordained deacon.

145 Leonard Maton, B.A., curate of Durrington, ordained deacon.

21 December 1623: ordained priest. [*AO, Conc. Test.*]

146 Thomas Durant, B.A., curate of St. Laurence's, Shaftesbury, Dors.,[1] ordained deacon.

21 December 1623: ordained priest. [*AO*]

147 Alexander Hyde,[2] LL.B., Fellow of New, Oxf., ordained deacon.

6 December 1634: rector of Wylye and Little Langford.[3] *Inst.* (f. 33) on the death of John Lee; patron, Philip, earl of Pembroke. *Comp.* (334/18 f. 141) 12 Feb. 1635; sureties, James Goldston, Giles Hazard.

19 May 1637: sub-dean of Salisbury. *Inst.* (f. 40) on the death of Giles Thornburgh; patron, the bishop.

5 January 1639: prebendary of Grantham Australis. *Inst.* (f. 45) on the cession of Humphrey Henchman; patron, the bishop. [*AO, DNB, FS*]

148 John Crosbie (Crosby), B.A., curate of Ludgershall, ordained deacon.

25 September 1625: curate of Chute, ordained priest. [*AO*]

149 Joseph Wright, B.A., curate of Longcot, Berks., ordained deacon.

11 September 1628: vicar of Buckland, Berks. *Inst.* (f. 24) on the death of Henry Bales; patron, Sir Edward Yate. *Comp.* (334/17 f. 170) 21 Nov. 1628; sureties, Walter Heywood, Richard Samuel. [*AO, WR*]

150 William Sellar, M.A. (Broadgates Hall, Oxf.), ordained deacon. [*ACO*]

151 Joseph Avery, M.A., curate of Ansty, ordained priest. [*AO*]

152 William Coomhayes, *litteratus*, curate of Okeford Fitzpaine, Dors., ordained deacon.

[*and see* nos. 89, 114]

10 June 1623
[*see* no. 42]

17 June 1623
[*see* no. 92]

18 June 1623
[*see* no. 18]

20 June 1623

153 Anthony (Arthur) Gulson, M.A., prebendary of Netheravon. *Inst.*

---

1 The church of St. Laurence, then a barn in Holy Trinity parish, was sold with its land in 1650: J. Hutchins, *Hist. of Dors.* ii. 30.

2 Bishop of Salisbury 1665–7.

3 Separate parishes *c.* 2 miles apart.

(f. 17) on the death of Thomas Heay; patron, the bishop. *Comp.* (334/16 f. 153); sureties, William Ireland, John Cooke. [*AC, FS*]

21 June 1623
154 George Pinckney, M.A., rector of Rushall. *Inst.* (f. 17) on the resignation of Robert Pinckney; patron, William Pinckney. *Comp.* (334/16 f. 150) 28 June 1623; sureties, Edward Tidcombe, Michael Tidcombe. [*AO, PR*]

9 July 1623
155 Richard Watts, M.A., rector of Pusey, Berks. *Inst.* (f. 18) on a death; patron, the Crown. *Comp.* (334/16 f. 154) 19 Aug. 1623; sureties, John Reynolds, Alexander Wimbisse. [? *ACO*]

16 July 1623
156 William Payne (Peyn),[1] S.T.B., rector of Easthampstead, Berks. *Inst.* (f. 18); patron, the Crown. [? *ACO*]

23 July 1623
[*see* no. 120]

27 July 1623
157 James Lesly, M.A., rector of Wasing, Berks. *Inst.* (f. 18) on a death; patron, the Crown.

16 August 1623
[*see* no. 127]

6 September 1623
158 George Ocham, M.A., licensed to preach.

21 September 1623
159 Luke Sutton, M.A., ordained deacon.
  19 December 1624: ordained priest. [*AC*]
160 Vincent Sparke, B.A., ordained priest. [*AO*]
161 Thomas Monteney, M.A. (Queens', Camb.), ordained deacon.
  19 September 1624: ordained priest. [*AC*]
[*and see* no. 83]

30 September 1623
162 Nicholas Waddington, M.A., rector of Luckington. *Inst.* (f. 18) on the death of Rhys Jones; patron, Robert Fitzherbert. *Comp.* (334/16 f. 160) 20 Nov. 1623; sureties, Jasper Waterhouse, Thomas Waterworth. [*AO, PR*]

3 October 1623
163 Henry Jennings (Jennens), *alumnus* of Oxford University, rector of Calstone Wellington. *Inst.* (f. 18) on the death of George Ferebee; patron, John Duckett. [*AO* (Jenkins), *PR*]

6 October 1623
[*see* no. 120]

---

[1] Cf. no. 45. It is possible to read Prynne in no. 45 and Payne in no. 156 as one and the same and possible that the Crown's presentment in 1623 was corroborative. Both possibilities seem remote.

10 November 1623
164 William Ringe,[1] M.A., rector of Landford. *Inst.* (f. 18) 13 Nov.; patron, John Stanton. [*AO*]

18 November 1623
165 Andrew Greaves, M.A., rector of Poulshot, licensed to preach in the diocese.
    28 May 1624: vicar of Westbury. No subscription or institution.[2] *Comp.* (334/17 f. 14); sureties, John Cooke, John Greene. [*AC*]

20 November 1623
166 Thomas Wathen, M.A., rector of Wasing, Berks. *Inst.* (f. 18) on a resignation; patron, the Crown. [*AO, WR* p. 373]

2 December 1623
167 William Hicks, M.A., prebendary of Torleton. *Inst.* (f. 18) on the resignation of Edward Davenant; patron, the bishop. [*AC, FS,*? *WR* p. 74]

5 December 1623
168 Thomas Ferebe (Fereby), M.A., vicar of Bishop's Cannings. *Inst.* (f. 18) on the death of George Ferebe; patron, John Ferebe. *Comp.* (334/17 f. 1) 31 Jan. 1624; sureties, Anthony Ferebe, Henry Gardner. [*AO, PR*]

13 December 1623
169 William Gallamore (Gallimore),[3] B.A., vicar of Swindon. *Inst.* (f. 18) on the resignation of Miles Kendal; patron, Thomas White. *Comp.* (334/17 f. 7) 12 Mar. 1624; sureties, Thomas White, Richard Constable. [*PR*]

21 December 1623
170 John Skeate, M.A., ordained deacon. [*AO*]
171 John Russell, B.A., ordained priest. [*AO*]
172 Anthony Hillary (Ellary), B.A. (Hart Hall, Oxf.), ordained deacon.
    18 December 1625: curate of Woodford, ordained priest.
    4 February 1633: vicar of St. Martin's, Salisbury. *Inst.* (f. 30); patron, the Crown.
    8 October 1635: rector of St. Martin's, Salisbury.[4] *Inst.* (f. 36); patron, John Bayly. *Comp.* (334/18 f. 231) 30 Apr. 1638; sureties, John Holt, Robert Squibb. [*AO, Conc. Test.*]
173 Rhys (Riceas) Jones (Johnes), B.A., ordained deacon. [*AO*]
174 Augustine Gauntlett, B.A., ordained priest. [*AO*]
175 David Feltham, B.A., ordained deacon.
    19 December 1624: ordained priest. [*AO* (Felton)]
176 Thomas Jackson, B.A., ordained deacon. [? *ACO*]
177 James Hawke, *litteratus*, ordained deacon.
[*and see* nos. 86, 112, 116, 119, 145–6]

---

[1] Cf. no. 116. It is possible, but not likely, that nos. 116 and 164 refer to the same man.
[2] Westbury was a peculiar of the precentor of Salisbury: *V.C.H. Wilts.* viii. 176.
[3] Cf. nos. 480, 556 and nn.
[4] St. Martin's was a vicarage from the early 13th century until 1635: *V.C.H. Wilts.* vi. 144–5.

23 February 1624
[*see* no. 127]

6 March 1624
[*see* no. 82]

9 March 1624
178 William Jay (Jeay), B.A., rector of Fittleton. *Inst.* (f. 19) on the death of Thomas Jay.[1] *Comp.* (334/17 f. 16) 7 June 1624; sureties, Thomas Jay, Thomas Jay.
19 September 1624: ordained priest. [*AO, PR, WR*]

15 March 1624
179 Edward Gough, M.A., rector of Great Cheverell. *Inst.* (f. 19) on the death of Griffin Williams; patron, Richard Goddard. *Comp.* (334/17 f. 7) 12 Mar. 1624; sureties, William Gough, William Norden.
8 May 1629: prebendary of Yatesbury. *Inst.* (f. 25) on the cession of Humphrey Henchman; patron, the bishop. *Comp.* (334/17 f. 197) 17 Oct. 1629; sureties, Francis Bennett, Edward May.
8 January 1634: licensed to preach in the diocese. [*AO, FS, PR*]

21 April 1624
180 John Sharpe, [B.A.,] prebendary of Horningsham and Tytherington. No subscription or institution.[2] *Comp.* (334/17 f. 9); sureties, Thomas Guy, John Lowes. [*AO*]

29 April 1624
[*see* no. 113]

4 May 1624
181 Thomas Atkinson, M.A., vicar of Overton. No subscription.[3] *Inst.* (f. 19) on the death of Thomas Clifford;[4] patron, Robert Veysey for William, earl of Pembroke. *Comp.* (334/17 f. 11) 30 Apr. 1624; sureties, William Batson, Walter Veysey. [? *ACO, PR*]

28 May 1624
[*see* no. 165]

24 June 1624
182 Richard Reeks, B.A., licensed to preach at Edington. [*WR* p. 318]

27 July 1624
[*see* no. 134]

25 August 1624
[*see* no. 34]

---

[1] A space is left in the institution book where details of the presentation usually appear.
[2] Although under his jurisdiction, the dean's book does not record Sharpe's subscription. Cf. nos. 217, 321.
[3] The reasons for Atkinson's failure to subscribe are not clear.
[4] Presumably a mistake for John Hayes (no. 131) who was instituted after Clifford's death.

4 September 1624
183 Michael Berwicke, B.A., licensed to preach at Ardington, Berks.
19 July 1625: vicar of Ardington. *Inst.* (f. 20) on the resignation of William Twisse; patrons, the dean and chapter of Christ Church, Oxford. [*AO*]

9 September 1624
184 Edmund Trewlocke, M.A., rector of St. Peter's, Wallingford, Berks. *Inst.* (f. 19) on the resignation of Bezaliel Burt; patron, the Crown. [*AO* (Trulocke)]

19 September 1624
185 Edward Collyer, B.A., ordained priest. [*AO*]
186 Christopher Reade, B.A., ordained deacon.
25 September 1625: curate of Netherhampton [Wilton parish], ordained priest. [*AO*]
187 Thomas Parker, *litteratus*, ordained priest.
188 Thomas Smith, B.A., ordained deacon. [? *AO*]
189 John Harding, B.A. (Exeter, Oxf.), curate of Melcombe Bingham, Dors., ordained deacon. [*AO*]
190 Silas Bushell, B.A. (Magdalen, Oxf.), ordained deacon.
13 March 1625: ordained priest. [*AO, WR* p. 129]
191 Henry Higgins, B.A. (Broadgates Hall, Oxf.), curate of Charlton, ordained deacon.
13 March 1625: ordained priest.
22 June 1631: licensed to preach in the diocese. [*AO*]
192 George Collier, B.A. (Gloucester Hall, Oxf.), curate of Steeple Langford, ordained priest. [*AO, WR* p. 310]
[*and see* nos. 82, 86, 161, 178]

9 October 1624
193 Henry Madgewicke, LL.B., rector of Allington. *Inst.* (f. 19) on the resignation of John South; patron, Sir Henry Wallop. *Comp.* (334/17 f. 26) 23 Oct. 1624; sureties, Gilbert Keate, George Turberville. [*AO, PR*]

16 October 1624
[*see* no. 119]

6 November 1624
194 Edward Roode, vicar of St. Helen's, Abingdon, Berks. *Inst.* (f. 19) on a resignation; patron, the Crown. *Comp.* (334/17 f. 30) 16 Nov. 1624; sureties, Thomas Quelye, William Shaffard.

25 November 1624
195 Robert Pocock (Pococke), M.A., rector of Brightwalton, Berks. *Inst.* (f. 19) on the death of Thomas Middleton; patron, William Chapman. *Comp.* (334/17 f. 35) 14 Dec. 1624; sureties, John Pococke, John Sawyer. [*AO*]

19 December 1624
196 Richard Swaine, B.A., ordained deacon.
18 December 1625: ordained priest. [*AO, WR* p. 137]

197 John Tyse, M.A., ordained deacon.

18 December 1625: ordained priest.

30 November 1638: rector of Orcheston St. George. *Inst.* (f. 44) on the death of Giles Thornburgh; patron, Edmund Lambert.

15 January 1639: rector of Orcheston St. George. *Inst.* (f. 46); patrons, Robert Tyse and Nicholas Goddard.[1] *Comp.* (334/20 f. 14) 7 May 1639; sureties, Thomas Alford, Giles Stagg. [*AO*]

198 Edward Fox, B.A., ordained priest. [*AO*]

199 Thomas King, B.A., ordained priest. [? *ACO*]

200 John Galping, B.A., ordained deacon.

18 December 1625: ordained priest. [*AO, CR* p. 216]

201 John Preston, B.A., ordained deacon. [*AO*]

202 Christopher Willan, B.A., ordained deacon.

18 December: curate of West Knoyle [North Newnton parish],[2] ordained priest. [*AO*]

203 John Pelling, B.A., curate of Staverton [Trowbridge parish], ordained deacon.

17 February 1627: ordained priest. [*AO*]

204 John Macham, B.A., ordained deacon. [*AO*]
[*and see* nos. 117, 159, 175]

13 January 1625
205 John Browning (Browninge), S.T.B., rector of Buttermere. *Inst.* (f. 20) on a death; patron, Lancelot, bishop of Winchester. *Comp.* (334/17 f. 43) 12 Apr. 1625; sureties, Ralph Durant, Thomas Dalley. [*AO, PR*]

14 January 1625
206 John Dawes, B.A., vicar of Market Lavington. *Inst.* (f. 19) on the death of Edmund Gwyn; patron, dean and chapter of Christ Church, Oxford. *Comp.* (334/17 f. 37) 31 Jan. 1625; sureties, Thomas Bennet, Thomas Sanford. [*AC*]

2 February 1625
207 Alan (Allan) Bishop, M.A., vicar of Ashton Keynes. *Inst.* (f. 20) on the death of John Hill; patron, Sir Thomas Sackville. *Comp.* (334/17 f. 42) 30 Mar. 1625; sureties, Richard Cornwall, Gabriel Goldney. [*AO, PR, WR*]

8 March 1625
208 Gabriel Bridges, M.A., rector of Ditteridge. *Inst.* (f. 20); patron, the Crown.

9 December 1636: rector of Letcombe Bassett, Berks. *Inst.* (f. 39) on the death of Robert Cullve; patron, Corpus Christi College, Oxford. *Comp.* (334/18 f. 191) 4 Feb. 1637; sureties, Thomas Bridges, William Seymour. [*AO, PR, WR* p. 277]

---

[1] Doubts about the right of presentation possibly led to Tyse's second institution. The Lamberts and Goddards were locally prominent families: *V.C.H. Wilts.* viii. 210–11, 253; ix, *passim.*

[2] For the dependence of West Knoyle as a chapelry on North Newnton see ibid. x. 133–5; and cf. no. 307 and nn.

13 March 1625
209 Hugh Atkins, *litteratus*, curate of All Cannings, ordained priest.
210 Samuel Quintin, B.A., curate of Odstock, ordained priest. [*AO*]
211 John Wright, *litteratus*, curate of Stone [Ham parish],[1] Glos., ordained deacon.
212 John Waterman, B.A., curate of Sopworth, ordained priest.
 6 December 1625: rector of Sopworth. *Inst.* (f. 21) on a resignation; patron, the Crown. *Comp.* (334/17 f. 68) 18 Jan. 1626; sureties, George Manshall, Thomas Hull.
[*and see* nos. 190–1]

6 April 1625
213 John Tone, S.T.B., rector of Kingston Bagpuze, Berks. *Inst.* (f. 20) on the death of George Raynsbie; patron, St. John's College, Oxford. *Comp.* (334/17 f. 44) 28 Apr. 1625; sureties, Peter Tone, William Griffin.

29 April 1625
214 Samuel Fowler, B.A., vicar of Stratton St. Margaret. *Inst.* (f. 20) on the resignation of William Fowler; patron, Merton College, Oxford. [*DNB, PR*]

3 May 1625
215 John Woodbridge, M.A., rector of Stanton.[2] *Inst.* (f. 20) on the death of William Edwards;[3] patron, Richard Organ. *Comp.* (334/17 f. 52) 29 June 1625; sureties, Godfrey Elder, Thomas Abbot. [*AO, DNB* (s.v. Benjamin Woodbridge), *PR*]

21 May 1625
216 Ellis Edwards, B.A., vicar of Liddington. *Inst.* (f. 20) on the death of William Edwards;[4] patron, Thomas Edwards. *Comp.* (334/17 f. 116) 14 Apr. 1627; sureties, Robert Harrison, George Ludlow. [*AO, PR*]

25 May 1625
217 Thomas Ailesbury (Aylesbury), M.A., rector of Berwick St. Leonard. *Inst.* (f. 20) 25 June 1625 on the death of William Poulton; patron, Sir Richard Grobham. *Comp.* (334/17 f. 62) 23 Nov. 1625; sureties, Edward Windover, George How.
 29 June 1631: prebendary of Horningsham and Tytherington. No subscription or institution.[5] *Comp.* (334/18 f. 20) 29 June 1631; sureties, Edward Love, John Gibbons. [*AC, PR, WR*]

27 June 1625
218 Thomas Marler, S.T.B., archdeacon of Salisbury. *Inst.* (f. 20) on the death of William Barlowe; patron, the bishop. *Comp.* (334/17 f. 86) 19 May 1626; sureties, Francis Kiblerosit, Robert Roberts. [*AO, FS, WR*]

---

[1] Stone was a chapelry of Ham: T. D. Fosbroke, *Glos.* i. 466.
[2] Stanton Fitzwarren: cf. no. 698.
[3] Cf. no. 216.   [4] Cf. no. 215.
[5] Although under his jurisdiction Ailesbury's subscription is not recorded in the dean's book. Cf. nos. 180, 321.

29 June 1625
219 Francis Allen, S.T.B., vicar of Kintbury, Berks. *Inst.* (f. 20) on the death of William Tarler; patron, Sir Anthony Hungerford. *Comp.* (334/17 f. 60) 9 Nov. 1625; sureties, Richard Mony, Hugh Horne. [*AO*]

6 July 1625
220 Thomas Morland, M.A., rector of Sulhampstead Abbots, Berks. *Inst.* (f. 20) on the death of John Wilkins; patron, Queen's College, Oxford. *Comp.* (334/17 f. 56) 15 July 1625; sureties, Richard Wintershull, Potans Brightwell. [*AO*]

19 July 1625
[*see* no. 183]

26 July 1625
221 John Astell, B.A. (Oxf.), rector of St. Leonard's, Wallingford, Berks. *Inst.* (f. 20) on a death; patron, the Crown. *Comp.* (334/17 f. 62) 23 Nov. 1625; sureties, Thomas Paine, John Paine. [*AO, PR*]

6 August 1625
222 Christopher Green (Greene), S.T.P., rector of Stockton. *Inst.* (f. 21) on a death; patron, Lancelot, bishop of Winchester. *Comp.* (334/17 f. 57) 6 Sept. 1625; sureties, Edward Greene, Richard Mattocks. [*ACO, PR, WR*]

16 August 1625
223 Roger Flower, M.A., rector of Little Cheverell. *Inst.* (f. 21) on the death of Hugh Gough;[1] patron, John Flower. *Comp.* (334/17 f. 61) 17 Nov. 1625; sureties, Giles Byrde, John Studleyde. [*AO, CR* p. 202, *PR*]

17 August 1625
224 Robert Bing (Byng), M.A., rector of All Cannings. *Inst.* (f. 21);[2] patron, Henry Byng. *Comp.* (334/17 f. 63) 26 Nov. 1625; sureties, Henry Bynge, Albert Fowler. [*AC, CR, WR*]

30 August 1625
225 Thomas Floid (Floyd, Lloyd), B.A., licensed to preach at Sutton Veny.
    5 August 1640: vicar of St. Lawrence's, Reading, Berks. *Inst.* (f. 49) on the death of Theophilus Taylor; patron, St. John's College, Oxford. [*AO*]

1 September 1625
226 Anthony Clopton, S.T.B., vicar of Stanford-in-the-Vale, Berks. *Inst.* (f. 21) on the death of Hugh Goodman; patrons, the dean and chapter of Westminster. *Comp.* (334/17 f. 90) 29 June 1626; sureties, Charles Townsend, George Townsend.
    15 March 1631: rector of Childrey, Berks. *Inst.* (f. 28) on the death of Christopher Membry; patron, Corpus Christi College, Oxford. *Comp.* (334/18 f. 11) 7 May 1631; sureties, Edward Trotman, George Raymond. [*AO*]

---

[1] Cf. no. 224 n.
[2] On the death of Hugh Gough (see no. 223): *V.C.H. Wilts.* x. 31, 59.

25 September 1625
227 William Squier,[1] B.A., ordained deacon. [*AO*, ? *WR* p. 190]
228 James Bandinell, M.A. (Christ Church, Oxf.), ordained deacon. [*AO*]
229 Thomas Rivers, B.A. (Magdalen, Oxf.), ordained deacon.
    23 September 1627: curate of Grateley, Hants, ordained priest. [*AO*]
230 George Raynolds, B.A. (Wadham, Oxf.), curate of Paultons [Eling parish], Hants, ordained deacon.
    17 February 1627: curate of Timsbury, Hants, ordained priest. [*AO*]
231 John Davis, B.A. (Christ Church, Oxf.), curate of Charlton, ordained deacon.
    23 September 1626: curate of Everleigh, ordained priest. [*AO*]
232 James Crouch, B.A. (All Souls', Oxf.), curate of Buckland Newton, Dors., ordained deacon. [*AO*, *WR* p. 131]
233 William Noyse, B.A. (Christ Church, Oxf.), curate of Sherfield English, Hants, ordained deacon.
    21 September 1628: curate of Wellow, Hants, ordained priest. [*AO*]
234 Francis Cuffley, B.A. (New Inn Hall, Oxf.), curate of Stanton by Highworth, ordained deacon. [*AO*]
235 Robert Tutt, M.A. (St. Edmund Hall, Oxf.), ordained deacon.
    28 August 1637: rector of Barford St. Martin. *Inst.* (f. 41) on the death of William Wilks; patron, John Bowles. *Comp.* (334/18 f. 219) 29 Nov. 1637; sureties, Richard Tutt, John Ryves. [*AO*, *FS*, *PR*, *WR*]
[*and see* nos. 148, 186]

11 October 1625
236 Edmund Tracie, M.A., licensed to preach at Warminster. [*AC* (Tracy), *WR*]

27 October 1625
237 Thomas Westly (Westley), M.A., vicar of Marcham, Berks. *Inst.* (f. 21); patron, the Crown. *Comp.* (334/17 f. 71) 28 Jan. 1626; sureties, Nicholas Orme, Simeon Orme. [*AO*, *WR* p. 321]

15 November 1625
238 William Webber, B.A., rector of St. Nicholas's, Abingdon, Berks. *Inst.* (f. 21) on a resignation; patron, the Crown. *Comp.* (334/17 f. 69) 23 Jan. 1626; sureties, William Burnham, John Charlton. [*AO*]

30 November 1625
239 James Jones, M.A., vicar of Clewer, Berks. *Inst.* (f. 21) on a resignation; patron, the Crown. *Comp.* (334/17 f. 70) 25 Jan. 1626; sureties, Christopher Corner, John Brumpsted. [*AO*]

6 December 1625
[*see* no. 212]

18 December 1625
240 Thomas Samwayes, B.A. (Gonville and Caius, Camb.), curate of

[1] Cf. no. 438 and n.

Owermoigne, Dors., ordained deacon.

20 September 1629: curate of Tincleton, Dors., ordained priest. [*AC*]

241 Timothy Chingron, B.A., ordained deacon. [*ACO*]

242 Thomas Freeman, M.A. (Oriel, Oxf.), ordained deacon.

31 May 1629: ordained priest. [*AO, WR* p. 173]

243 George Tarrant, M.A., ordained deacon. [*AO*]

244 John Fordham, M.A., curate of Melksham, ordained deacon. [*AO*]

245 John Reade, B.A. (Balliol, Oxf.), ordained deacon.

20 September 1629: licensed at Calbourne, Isle of Wight, ordained priest.[1]

3 March 1630: curate of St. Edmund's, Salisbury. [*AO*]

246 David Comage, B.A. (Exeter, Oxf.), ordained deacon.

31 May 1629: curate of Winterslow, ordained priest. [*AO*]

247 Joseph Rose, *litteratus*, ordained deacon.[2]

[*and see* nos. 172, 196–7, 200, 202]

31 December 1625

248 John White, licensed to preach at Wylye and in the diocese. [? *ACO*][3]

18 January 1626

[*see* no. 48]

26 January 1626

249 Thomas Powell, vicar of Britford. No subscription or institution.[4]
Comp. (334/17 f. 70); sureties, Edward Field, Richard Field. [? *ACO*]

31 January 1626

[*see* no. 40]

6 February 1626

250 Edward Hyde, S.T.B., rector of West Grimstead with Plaitford.[5]
Inst. (f. 21) on the death of Richard Wall; patron, William South. *Comp.*
(334/17 f. 81) 21 Apr. 1626; sureties, Gilbert Richards, Robert Hunter.
[*AO, PR, WR*]

1 March 1626

251 John Ryves, LL.B., prebendary of Gillingham Major. *Inst.* (f. 21) on
the death of Aesop Clive; patron, the bishop.

20 November 1634: archdeacon of Berkshire. *Inst.* (f. 33) on the resignation of Edward Davenant; patron, the bishop. *Comp.* (334/18 f. 138)
29 Nov. 1634; sureties, John Fussel, Leonard Welstead. [*AO, FS, WR*
pp. 136–7]

9 March 1626

252 Joseph Nixon, S.T.B., rector of Ashbury, Berks. *Inst.* (f. 21) on the death
of Edmund Culpepper; patron, Sir Henry Marten. *Comp.* (334/17 f. 80)

[1] Reade's licence was probably to preach but that was not stated in his subscription.
[2] The subscription is incomplete and unsigned but was apparently made 18 Dec.
[3] Possibly son of John White, rector of Holy Trinity, Dorchester, Dors.: *D.N.B.*
[4] Britford was a peculiar of the dean and chapter of Salisbury but Powell's subscription is not recorded in the dean's book.
[5] Plaitford was a chapelry of West Grimstead: Hoare, *Mod. Wilts.* Frustfield, 96.

31 March 1626; sureties, Thomas Potter, Benjamin Potter.

4 February 1637: rector of Buttermere. *Inst.* (f. 39); patron, Walter, bishop of Winchester. *Comp.* (334/18 f. 197) 13 Mar. 1637; sureties, Thomas Boyland, Ralph Keable. [*AO, WR*]

15 March 1626
253 Thomas Woods, M.A., rector of Buttermere. *Inst.* (f. 22) on the resignation of John Browning; patron, Lancelot, bishop of Winchester. *Comp.* (334/17 f. 80) 8 Apr. 1626; sureties, Henry Tomes, John Heywood. [*AC, PR*]

25 March 1626
254 Edward Ceney, M.A., vicar of Warfield, Berks. *Inst.* (f. 22) on the death of Roger Tacker; patron, Henry Brabourne. *Comp.* (334/17 f. 86) 19 May 1626; sureties, Arthur Garforde, Edward Grage. [*AC* (Chinay)]

28 March 1626
255 John Willis, M.A., rector of East Coulston. *Inst.* (f. 22) 18 Apr. 1626 on the resignation of Henry Moore; patron, the Crown. *Comp.* (334/17 f. 88) 9 June 1626; sureties, Roger Hill, Griffin Powell.

22 June 1632: vicar of North Bradley and Southwick.[1] *Inst.* (f. 30) on the death of Matthew Jervis; patron, Winchester College. *Comp.* (334/18 f. 61) 18 Aug. 1632; sureties, William Parker, Thomas Parker.

8 January 1634: licensed to preach in the diocese. [*AO, PR*]

9 May 1626
256 Robert Pearson,[2] S.T.P., prebendary of Netheravon. *Inst.* (f. 22) on the death of Anthony Gulson; patron, the bishop. *Comp.* (334/17 f. 89) 19 June 1626; sureties. Gilbert Richards, Richard Bisbie. [*AC, FS*]

1 June 1626
257 Peter Seaman, M.A., vicar of Charlton. *Inst.* (f. 22) on a death; patron, the dean and chapter of Christ Church, Oxford. [*AO, PR*]

13 June 1626
258 Laurence Pocock (Pococke), M.A., rector of Brightwalton, Berks. *Inst.* (f. 22) on the death of Robert Pococke; patron, William Chapman. *Comp.* (334/17 f. 93) 22 July 1626; sureties, John Hatt, Thomas Hatt. [*AO*]

14 June 1626
259 Thomas Lecey *alias* Hedges (Hodges), M.A., vicar of Rodbourne Cheney. *Inst.* (f. 22) on the death of Anthony Ellis; patron, William Lecey *alias* Hedges. *Comp.* (334/17 f. 92) 13 July 1626; sureties, John Lowe, William Lucas.

22 September 1634: licensed to preach in the diocese. [*AO, PR*]

21 July 1626
260 John Wilson, B.A., vicar of Bishopstone. *Inst.* (f. 22) on the cession of Thomas Powell; patron, John Barnston. [? *ACO, PR, WR*]

---

[1] Southwick was in the ecclesiastical parish of North Bradley: *V.C.H. Wilts.* viii. 218.

[2] John Pearson, prebendary of Netheravon (no. 800), was Robert's son.

17 August 1626
261 Charles Deane, M.A., vicar of Waltham St. Lawrence, Berks. *Inst.* (f. 22) on the death of Peter Fawkner; patron, Sir Henry Newill. [*AO*, *WR* p. 172]

2 September 1626
262 Henry Hulbert, M.A., rector of Hilperton. *Inst.* (f. 22) on the death of William Buckle; patron, Thomas Horne. *Comp.* (334/17 f. 104) 22 Nov. 1626; sureties, Millicentius Dorman, Richard Perkins. [*AO*, *PR*]

12 September 1626
263 John Royston, M.A., rector of Shaw, Berks. *Inst.* (f. 22) on the death of Francis Tomlinson; patron, Humphrey Dolman. *Comp.* (334/17 f. 97) 23 Sept. 1626; sureties, Abraham Haynes, Robert Benbowe.

18 September 1626
264 Anthony Saunders, M.A., rector of Pangbourne, Berks. *Inst.* (f. 22) on the death of Thomas Pearson; patron, John Saunders. *Comp.* (334/17 f. 104) 21 Nov. 1626; sureties, John Saunders, William Clement. [*AO*]

23 September 1626
265 Thomas Davis, B.A. (Pembroke, Oxf.), curate of East Coulston, ordained deacon.
  22 December 1627: ordained priest. [*AO*]
266 Thomas Bisson, B.A., curate of Upavon, ordained deacon. [*AO*, *Conc. Test.*, *WR* p. 369]
267 Edward Deare, B.A., curate of Barford St. Martin, ordained deacon.
  17 February 1627: ordained priest. [*AO*]
268 Samuel Michell (Mitchell), B.A. (Magdalen, Oxf.), ordained deacon.
  3 March 1632: vicar of Latton. *Inst.* (f. 29) on the death of Randall Ashton; patron, John Slade. [*AO*]
269 Matthew Rendall, M.A. (Oxf.), ordained deacon.
  17 February 1627: ordained priest.
270 Nicholas Smith, M.A., curate of Gillingham, Dors., ordained priest. [? *ACO*]
[*and see* no. 231]

27 September 1626
271 Francis Matkin (Mackyn), LL.B., prebendary of Warminster. *Inst.* (f. 22) on the resignation of Edward Evans; patron, the bishop. *Comp.* (334/17 f. 102) 14 Nov. 1626; sureties, Roger Ludlowe, Richard Blake. [*AO*, *FS*, *WR* pp. 187, 377]

13 October 1626
272 George Bayly (Balaeus), [B.D.,] rector of Cricklade St. Mary. *Inst.* (f. 22) on a death; patrons, Roger Burgoyne, Robert Straunge, Robert Oldisworth, and John Burgoyne. [*AO*, *PR*]

24 October 1626
273 John Keat, M.A., licensed to preach in the diocese. [? *AO*]

15 November 1626
274 Thomas Moore, S.T.B., rector of Buttermere. *Inst.* (f. 22) on a death;[1] patron, the Crown.[2] *Comp.* (334/17 f. 105) 25 Nov. 1626; sureties, Matthew Bateson, Ralph Slater. [? *ACO, PR*]

21 December 1626
275 Thomas Godwyn, S.T.B., rector of Brightwell, Berks. *Inst.* (f. 23) on a death; patron, the Crown. *Comp.* (334/17 f. 109) 2 Jan. 1627; sureties, Brian Cole, Edward Palmer. [*AO, DNB* (Godwin)]

3 January 1627
276 Michael Becke, M.A., licensed to preach in the diocese. [*AO*]

17 February 1627
277 Richard Hyde, M.A. (Oriel, Oxf.), ordained deacon.
    2 March 1634: ordained priest. [*AO, FS, PR, WR* pp. 374–5]
278 Richard Yeomans, B.A., curate of Ditteridge, ordained priest. [*AO*]
279 Henry Smith, B.A., curate of Chute, ordained deacon.
    21 September 1628: curate of Ludgershall, ordained priest. [? *ACO*]
280 John Evans, B.A., curate of Bindon [Wool parish], Dors., ordained priest. [? *ACO*]
281 Arthur Warwick, B.A. (Magdalen, Oxf.), ordained deacon.
    21 September 1628: curate of Burley, Hants, ordained priest. [*AO*]
282 William Batchelour, B.A., curate of Inglesham, ordained deacon. [*AO* (Bachelor)]
[*and see* nos. 203, 230, 267, 269]

23 February 1627
[*see* no. 26]

5 March 1627
[*see* no. 68]

24 March 1627[3]
283 Richard Long, M.A., vicar of Winterbourne Monkton. *Inst.* (f. 23) 14 Mar. 1627 on a death; patron, the Crown. [*PR, WR* p. 316]

15 March 1627
284 Roger Powell, B.A., licensed to preach in the diocese. [*AO, Conc. Test.*]

24 May 1627
285 John Williamson, S.T.B., vicar of Sparsholt, Berks. *Inst.* (f. 23) on the death of Thomas Todhunter; patron, Queen's College, Oxford. *Comp.* (334/17 f. 123) 30 May 1627; sureties, Nicholas Williamson, Christopher Batman. [*AO*]

30 May 1627
286 William Palmer, vicar of Hilmarton, licensed to preach. *Inst.* (f. 23) on

---

1 Presumably that of Thomas Woods: no. 253.
2 On a vacancy of the see of Winchester: cf. no. 253.
3 The date of this subscription is possibly a mistake for 14 Mar. since otherwise it stands out of chronological order in the book.

a death; patron, the Crown. *Comp.* (334/17 f. 142) 5 Feb. 1628; sureties, William Shute, William Nott. [*PR*]

1 June 1627
287 Stephen Rose, M.A., vicar of Aldermaston, Berks. *Inst.* (f. 23) on the death of George Bradshawe; patron, Sir Humphrey Forster. *Comp.* (334/17 f. 123) 31 May 1627; sureties, William Barlowe, Thomas Packer.

    27 February 1633: rector of Barkham, Berks. *Inst.* (f. 30) 17 Feb. 1633 on the death of Richard Pridyat; patron, William Standon.

    16 January 1640: rector of Arborfield, Berks. No subscription or institution.[1] *Comp.* (334/20 f. 41); sureties, Robert Bostock, Edward Peace. [*AO*]

21 June 1627
288 John Wilkinson, S.T.P., rector of Tubney, Berks. *Inst.* (f. 23) on the resignation of Francis Bradshawe; patron, Magdalen College, Oxford. [*AO*]

7 July 1627
[*see no.* 28]

23 July 1627
289 Bernard Waight, M.A., vicar of Minety. *Inst.* (f. 23) on the death of Thomas Morgan; patron, Thomas Long.[2] [*AO* (Wayte)]

23 September 1627
290 John Arody, B.A. (Merton, Oxf.) ordained deacon.
291 Henry Symes, B.A. (Trinity, Oxf.), ordained deacon. [*AO*]
292 Timothy Richards, M.A. (Brasenose, Oxf.), ordained deacon.

    25 February 1629: vicar of Rowde. *Inst.* (f. 25) on the death of Dominus Tice; patron, Edward Baynton. [*AO, Conc. Test., PR*]
293 Samuel Tyrer, B.A. (St. Alban Hall, Oxf.), ordained deacon.
294 Nicholas Clarke, M.A., curate of Gillingham, Dors., ordained priest. [*AO*]
[*and see* no. 229]

4 November 1627
295 John Hungerford, [M.A.,] rector of Hazelbury.[3] *Inst.* (f. 23); patron, the Crown. [*AO, DNB, PR*]

13 December 1627
296 Thomas Stanford (Stamford), [M.A.,] rector of Castle Eaton. *Inst.* (f. 23) on the death of William Smith; patron, Edward Goddard. *Comp.* (334/17 f. 141) 23 Jan. 1628; sureties, Richard Birde, William Childe.

    8 June 1628: ordained priest. [*AC, PR*]

---

[1] Arborfield was a peculiar of the dean of Salisbury before whom Rose subscribed 17 Dec. 1639.
[2] Cf. no. 305.
[3] Hazlebury remained a separate living although by 1783 the church had been demolished: *Returns to Visitation Queries 1783*, ed. Mary Ransome (W.R.S. xxvii), p. 22 n. In the 19th cent. Hazlebury was in Box parish.

22 December 1627
297 William Kintell, M.A. (Magdalen, Oxf.), ordained deacon.

18 December 1631: curate of Bratton [Westbury parish], ordained priest.
298 Thomas Sclater, B.A. (St. Edmund Hall, Oxf.), ordained deacon.
[*AO*, *WR* p. 319]
299 James White, B.A. (Clare, Camb.), ordained deacon.

10 August 1629: prebendary of Hurstbourne and Burbage. *Inst.* (f. 26) on
the death of William Prichard; patron, the bishop. *Comp.* (334/17 f. 198)
23 Oct. 1629; sureties, William Ireland, Valentine Petit.

6 June 1632: rector of Boscombe. *Inst.* (f. 29) on the death of John
Thorpe; patron, the bishop. *Comp.* (334/18 f. 63) 6 Oct. 1632; sureties,
Valentine Petit, George Parker.

28 March 1638: rector of Rollestone. *Inst.* (f. 43) on a cession;[1] patron,
the Crown. *Comp.* (334/18 f. 230) 26 Apr. 1638; sureties, Valentine Petit,
George Parker. [*AC*, *FS*, *WR*]
300 Thomas Prynne, B.A. (Oriel, Oxf.), ordained deacon. [*AO*]
301 Edward Cleaver, M.A. (Pembroke, Oxf.), ordained deacon.

21 September 1628: ordained priest.[2] [? *AO*]
[*and see* no. 265]

23 December 1627[3]
302 Edward Winley, B.A. (Magdalen, Oxf.), ordained deacon.

16 January 1628
303 John Robinson, M.A., vicar of Sunninghill in Windsor Forest. *Inst.*
(f. 23) on a resignation; patron, St. John's College, Cambridge. [*AO*]

25 January 1628
304 Robert Foster, M.A., rector of Foxley. *Inst.* (f. 23) on the death of
Richard Faine; patron, John Ayliffe. [*AC*, *PR*]

9 February 1628
[*see* no. 68]

23 February 1628
305 James Welsh (Wealsh), B.A., vicar of Minety. *Inst.* (f. 24) 13 Feb. 1628
on the death of Thomas Morgan;[4] patrons, Philip Langley, Robert Paget.
[*AO*, *PR*, *WR* pp. 381–2]
306 Ellis (Elizeas) Lawrence, M.A., rector of Semley. *Inst.* (f. 24) 13 Feb.
1628 on the death of Thomas Lawrence; patron, Daniel Yarde. *Comp.*

---

1 Presumably that of Christopher Tesdale: no. 512.
2 The difficulties in reading the proper names in the subscriptions of 1627 and 1628 leave
a doubt that they were by the same man. The similarity in the hands lessens, but does
not quite remove, the doubt.
3 The date is possibly a mistake for 22 Dec. but more likely Winley's subscription was
taken late.
4 Bernard Waight was instituted vicar 23 July 1627 on Morgan's death: no. 289. Welsh's
institution was possibly on Waight's death or possibly followed a challenge of Thomas
Long's right of patronage.

(334/17 f. 141) 31 Jan. 1628: sureties, Richard Carles, Richard Harbie. [*AO, PR*]

24 February 1628
[*see* no. 46]

6 March 1628
307 Thomas Chaffin (Chafin), M.A., prebendary of North Newnton.[1] *Inst.* (f. 24) on the death of Thomas Morgan; patron, William, earl of Pembroke.

7 March 1629: rector of Fovant. *Inst.* (f. 25) on the death of William Leonard; patron, William, earl of Pembroke. *Comp.* (334/18 f. 214) 31 Mar. 1630; sureties, Francis Chaffin, Thomas Bodnell.

9 February 1633: vicar of Mere. No subscription or institution.[2] *Comp.* (334/18 f. 76); sureties, Francis Chafin, John Butler.

3 July 1633: prebendary of Little Knoyle. No subscription or institution. *Comp* (334/18 f. 91); sureties, Francis Chafin, John Brittox.[3] [*AO, PR, WR*]

11 March 1628
308 Tobias Potter, S.T.B., rector of Binfield, Berks. *Inst.* (f. 24) on a death; patron, the Crown. *Comp.* (334/17 f. 145); sureties, Richard Peace, Henry Fisher. [*AO*]

21 May 1628
309 William Dillon, LL.B., vicar of Steventon, Berks. *Inst.* (f. 24) on a death; patron, John, bishop of Lincoln. [*AO, WR*, p. 278]

2 June 1628
310 Jeffrey Godwin, vicar of Froxfield. *Inst.* (f. 24) on the cession of Laomedon Fowler; patrons, the dean and chapter of Windsor.

22 September 1628: ordained priest.

29–31 May 1635:[4] licensed to preach in the diocese. [*PR*]

5 June 1628
311 William Seaman, M.A., rector of Upton Scudamore. *Inst.* (f. 24) on the death of James Langley; patron, William Seaman.[5] *Comp.* (334/17 f. 156) 26 June 1628; sureties, Gabriel Cox, senior, Gabriel Cox, junior.

8 June 1628: ordained priest. [*AO, DNB, PR*]

---

[1] North Newnton had been a prebend in Wilton Abbey: *V.C.H. Wilts.* x. 133. Chaffin described the prebend, with no cathedral stall, as 'ruralem'.

[2] Mere was a peculiar of the dean of Salisbury before whom Chaffin subscribed 18 July 1630.

[3] West (Little) Knoyle was a chapelry of the prebend and vicarage of North Newnton: *V.C.H. Wilts.* x. 133–5. It is not clear why Chaffin compounded in 1633 unless it is the compounding for the prebend of North Newnton to which he was instituted, but for which he did not compound, in 1628. There was a similarly long delay in his compounding for Mere.

[4] The position in the book of this subscription, which is undated, is a rough indication of its date.

[5] Apparently the subscriber himself. The advowson was acquired by The Queen's College, Oxford, in 1766: *V.C.H. Wilts.* viii. 86. The statement in *D.N.B.* that the college held it earlier is incorrect.

8 June 1628

312 Peter Vincent, M.A. (Queens', Camb.), ordained priest. [*AC*]

313 John Straight, M.A. (Queens', Camb.), ordained deacon.

21 December 1628: ordained priest. [*AC*]

314 Edmund Duddell, B.A. (Brasenose, Oxf.), curate of Bemerton [Fugglestone parish], ordained priest. [*AO*]

315 Edward Bannister, M.A. (Hart Hall, Oxf.), ordained deacon.

31 May 1629: ordained priest. [*AO*]

[*and see* nos. 296, 311]

12 July 1628

316 Thomas Janney (Jenney), M.A., vicar of West Hanney, Berks. *Inst.* (f. 24) on a death; patron, Henry Seaward. *Comp.* (334/17 f. 169) 15 Nov. 1628; sureties, Anthony Long, John Parham. [*AC*]

10 September 1628

317 William Combe, M.A., vicar of Hannington. *Inst.* (f. 24) on the death of Richard Stubbs; patron, Richard Swayne. [? *AO, PR*]

11 September 1628

[*see* no. 149]

21 September 1628

318 William Pinck, M.A. (Magdalen, Oxf.), ordained priest. [*AO*]

319 Francis Mercer, M.A. (Trinity, Camb.), ordained deacon. [*AC*]

320 William Bisco, M.A. (King's, Camb.), ordained priest. [*FS*]

321 Philip Hunton, B.A. (Wadham, Oxf.), ordained priest.

13 February 1632: prebendary of Horningsham and Tytherington. No subscription or institution.[1] *Comp.* (334/18 f. 41); sureties, William Rolfe, Thomas Carter.

27 December 1638: licensed to preach at St. John's and St. Mary's, Devizes.[2] [*AO, CR* p. 285, *DNB*]

322 John Newby, M.A. (Magdalen, Oxf.), ordained priest. [*AO*]

323 John Imber, B.A. (Winchester College and former Fellow of New, Oxf.), ordained deacon. [*AO* (Imbar), *WR* p. 185]

324 Henry Bellingham, B.A. (Magdalen, Oxf.), curate of Romsey, Hants, ordained deacon. [*AO*]

325 Thomas King, B.A. (Hart Hall, Oxf.), ordained deacon.

20 September 1629: ordained priest. [*AO*]

326 Ralph Ironside, M.A. (Magdalen, Oxf.), ordained priest. [*AO, FS, WR* p. 134]

327 Henry South, M.A. (St. Edmund Hall, Oxf.), ordained priest. [*AO*]

[*and see* nos. 233, 279, 281, 301]

22 September 1628

[*see* no. 310]

---

[1] Cf. nos. 180 and n., 217 and n. Hunton subscribed before the dean 13 Oct. 1631.

[2] Hunton was a zealous adherent of Cromwell: *D.N.B.* He was possibly licensed at Devizes, where the rectory was poorly endowed (*V.C.H. Wilts.* x. 286), to give the town the services of an able preacher.

12 November 1628
328 John Chenell (Channell), M.A., vicar of Beedon, Berks. *Inst.* (f. 24) on the death of William Wolse; patron, Edward Weston. [*AO*]

19 December 1628
329 Humphrey Newbury, B.A., vicar of Waltham St. Lawrence, Berks.[1] *Inst.* (f. 25); patron, Sir Henry Nevill. [*AO*]

21 December 1628
330 Nathaniel Steevans, M.A. (Magdalen, Oxf.), curate of Stanton St. Bernard,[2] ordained deacon.

23 May 1630: curate of Charburton [Charminster parish], Dors., ordained priest. [*AO* (Stephens), *CR* p. 462, *DNB*]
331 James Doherty, M.A. (Marischall's, Aberdeen),[3] curate of Owermoigne, Dors., ordained deacon.

31 May 1629: ordained priest.
332 Adiel Baynard (Baynarde), M.A. (Balliol, Oxf.), ordained deacon. [*AO* (Barnard), *WR* p. 145]
333 Marcus Zeigler (Exeter, Oxf.), curate of West Grimstead, ordained deacon.

19 September 1630: ordained priest. [*AO*]
334 Thomas Saie, B.A. (Magdalen, Oxf.), curate of Newton [Buckland parish], Berks., ordained deacon. [*AO* (Sayer)]
335 Christopher Ford (Forde), B.A. (Hart Hall, Oxf.), ordained deacon.

22 December 1633: curate of Compton Chamberlayne, ordained priest.

23 January 1635: vicar of Compton Chamberlayne. *Inst.* (f. 33) on the death of John Duggesmore; patron, John Penruddock. [*AO*]
[*and see* no. 313]

29 December 1628
336 Bartholomew Shapley (Shepley, Shipley), M.A., rector of Pusey, Berks. *Inst.* (f. 25) on the death of Richard Bale; patron, the bishop. *Comp.* (334/17 f. 186) 16 May 1629; sureties, Roger Pearde, Benedict Gregory.

19 September 1640: prebendary of Winterbourne Earls. No subscription.[4] *Inst.* (f. 49) on the death of Henry Edwards; patron, the bishop. [*AO, FS, WR*]

28 January 1629
337 Richard Hawes, M.A., vicar of Cookham, Berks. *Inst.* (f. 25) 18 Jan. 1629 on the death of John Vernon; patron, Humphrey Newbury. *Comp.* (334/17 f. 181) 31 Mar. 1629; sureties, Josiah Fendall, John Talbot. [*AO*]

---

[1] Cf. no. 455 and n.
[2] Where his father Richard was vicar: *D.N.B.*
[3] Doherty is the only subscribing ordinand known to have graduated in Scotland although there were other graduates of Scottish universities in the diocese: e.g. James Wedderburne, no. 426.
[4] The last recorded subscription before Davenant is dated 5 Aug. 1640.

31 January 1629
338 Thomas Bunbury (Bunburye), M.A., rector of St. Mary's, Reading, Berks. *Inst.* (f. 25) on a death; patron, the Crown. *Comp.* (334/17 f. 179) 14 Mar. 1629; sureties, John Bunbury, Thomas Rogers. [*AO, WR*]

25 February 1629
[*see* no. 292]

27 February 1629
[*see* no. 125]

5 March 1629
339 John King, S.T.P., rector of Remenham, Berks. *Inst.* (f. 25) on a resignation; patron, Sir Richard Lovelace. *Comp.* (334/17 f. 184) 9 May 1629; sureties, Richard King, John Clarke. [*AO, DNB*]

7 March 1629
340 Gilbert Hinde (Hynde), M.A., vicar of Streatley, Berks. *Inst.* (f. 25) on the death of William Beekesdale; patron, the bishop. *Comp.* (334/17 f. 182) 17 Apr. 1629; sureties, William Ireland, John Stogdell.

28 March 1632: rector of Aston Tirrold, Berks. *Inst.* (f. 29) on the resignation of John Bradford; patron, Magdalen College, Oxford. *Comp.* (334/18 f. 46) 14 Apr. 1632; sureties, William Ireland, John Stogdell.

26 July 1636: prebendary of Beaminster Prima. *Inst.* (f. 38) on the death of Robert Pinckney; patron, the bishop. *Comp.* (334/18 f. 184) 20 Oct. 1636; sureties, John Stogdell, James Holland. [*AO, FS, WR*]
[*and see* no. 307]

21 March 1629
[*see* no. 137]

28 March 1629
341 Tobias Crispe, M.A., rector of Brinkworth. *Inst.* (f. 25) on the death of Edward Hutchins; patrons, Rowland Wilson and Nicholas Crispe. *Comp.* (334/17 f. 182) 17 Apr. 1629; sureties, Samuel Crispe, Francis Cooke. [*ACO, DNB, PR*]

30 March 1629
342 John Thorpe, S.T.B., prebendary of Chute and Chisenbury. *Inst.* (f. 25) on the death of Edward Hutchins; patron, the bishop. *Comp.* (334/17 f. 182) 16 Apr. 1629; sureties, Edward Henchman, Maurice Henchman.

26 October 1630: rector of Boscombe. *Inst.* (f. 28) on the death of Edward Hyde; patron, the bishop. *Comp.* (334/18 f. 23) 26 July 1631; sureties, William Ireland, John Stogdell. [*AC, FS*]

8 May 1629
[*see* no. 179]

12 May 1629
343 John Wilton, M.A., rector of Great Chalfield. *Inst.* (f. 25) on the death of Robert Bradshaw; patron, William Eyre. [*AO, PR*]

31 May 1629
344 William Latymer, B.A. (Magdalen, Oxf.), curate of Dauntsey, ordained priest.
  7 July 1633: vicar of St. Paul's, Malmesbury. *Inst.* (f. 31) on a resignation; patron, the Crown. [*AO*]
345 Nathaniel Conduit, M.A. (Wadham, Oxf.), ordained deacon.
  24 December 1637: ordained priest. [*AO*]
346 William Hayter, B.A. (Trinity, Oxf.), ordained deacon.
  1 June 1634: ordained priest. [*AO*]
347 Robert Turner, M.A. (St. Edmund Hall, Oxf.), ordained deacon. [*AO*]
348 Thomas Sambourne, B.A. (Magdalen, Oxf.), ordained deacon.
  21 February 1630: ordained priest. [*AO*, *WR* p. 190]
349 Samuel Byrd, B.A. (St. Alban Hall, Oxf.), ordained priest.
350 William Vaughan, M.A. (Queens', Camb.) ordained priest. [*AC*]
[*and see* nos. 242, 246, 315, 331]

2 June 1629
351 Robert Peyton, S.T.B., vicar of Broad Chalke. *Inst.* (f. 25) on the death of Walter Waller; patron, King's College, Cambridge. *Comp.* (334/17 f. 190) 30 June 1629; sureties, Sir Edward Peyton, John Peyton. [*AC*, *PR*]

24 June 1629
352 Christopher Newstead, M.A., vicar of St. Helen's, Abingdon, Berks. No subscription.[1] *Inst.* (f. 26) on the deprivation of Edward Roades; patron, the Crown. [*AO*, *DNB*]

... June 1629[2]
353 James Halsey, M.A., rector of Buttermere. No subscription.[3] *Inst.* (f. 26) on the resignation of Thomas Moore; patron, [Richard,] bishop of Winchester. [*AO*, *PR*]

9 July 1629
354 Richard Heighmore, B.A. (Balliol, Oxf.), curate of Clifton Maybank, Dors., ordained deacon.
  20 September 1629: ordained priest. [*AO*]

31 July 1629
355 George Ditton, B.A., vicar of Chitterne St. Mary. *Inst.* (f. 26) on the death of Anthony Lyne; patron, Jordan Slade. [*AO* (Dilton), *PR*]

10 August 1629
[*see* no. 299]

16 September 1629
[*see* no. 15]

17 September 1629
356 Thomas Allcock, M.A., vicar of Broad Hinton. *Inst.* (f. 26) on the

---

[1] It is not clear why Newstead's subscription is not recorded.
[2] The day of the month cannot be read with certainty.
[3] It is not clear why Halsey's subscription is not recorded.

cession of John Northey; patron, Edward Northey. *Comp.* (334/17 f. 203) 21 Nov. 1629; sureties, Edward Northey, Anthony Neate. [*AC, PR*]

20 September 1629
357 Thomas Smart, Scholar of Hart Hall, Oxf., B.A., curate of Castle Eaton, ordained deacon.
19 September 1630: ordained priest.
358 Andrew Cox, B.A. (Magdalen, Oxf.), curate of Lovington, Som., ordained deacon. [*AO*]
359 George Luttrell, Scholar of Wadham, Oxf., curate of Stratford Tony, ordained deacon.
[*and see* nos. 240, 245, 325, 354]

19 October 1629
360 William Alford, M.A., vicar of Purton. *Inst.* (f. 26) on the death of James Hungerford; patron, Sir John Cooper. *Comp.* (334/17 f. 202) 14 Nov. 1629; sureties, Edward Alford, Laurence Pay. [*AO, PR*]

23 October 1629
361 Anthony Cooley,[1] rector of Huish. *Inst.* (f. 26) on the death of John Cooley; patron, William Seymour, earl of Hertford. *Comp.* (334/17 f. 203) 24 Nov. 1629; sureties, Thomas Guy, Simon Andrews. [*AO, PR*]

19 December 1629
362 Henry Norbonne, M.A. (St. Alban Hall, Oxf.), ordained deacon.
14 October 1637: rector of Langley Burrell. *Inst.* (f. 42) on the death of Mr. Berry; patron, Henry White. *Comp.* (334/18 f. 212) 21 Oct. 1637; sureties, Richard Ledesham, John Bonner.
24 December 1637: ordained priest.
24 February 1638: rector of Yatesbury. *Inst.* (f. 42) on the death of Peter Riche; patron, Sir Edward Baynton. *Comp.* (334/18 f. 230) 20 Apr. 1638; sureties, Richard Ledesham, John Bonner. [*AO, WR*]
363 Randolph Calcott, M.A. (Magdalen, Oxf.), ordained deacon.
21 December 1630: ordained priest. [*AO* (Caldecott), *PR*]
364 Leonard Clotworthie,[2] B.A. (New Inn Hall, Oxf.), curate of Poole,[3] ordained deacon. [*AO*]
365 Francis Lewis, B.A. (Lincoln, Oxf.), curate of Bratton [Westbury parish], ordained deacon.
19 December 1630: ordained priest. [*AO, WR* pp. 281–2]
366 Gabriel Sangar, B.A. (Magdalen, Oxf.), ordained deacon.
6 December 1630: rector of Sutton Mandeville. *Inst.* (f. 28) on the death of Thomas Sangar; patron, Gabriel Estgate. *Comp.* (334/18 f. 10) 21 Apr. 1631; sureties, Robert Chambers, Robert Woodford.
5 June 1631: ordained priest. [*AO, CR* p. 427]
367 Hugh Jones, B.A. (Magdalen, Oxf.), curate of Lymington, Hants, ordained deacon.
21 February 1630: ordained priest. [*AO*]

[1] Cooley matriculated but apparently did not graduate: *AO*.
[2] Cf. no. 727 and n.   [3] Probably Poole Keynes, but possibly Poole, Dors.

7 January 1630
368 John Sampson, [M.A.,] vicar of Blewbury, Berks. No subscription or institution.[1] *Comp.* (334/17 f. 207); sureties, John Loveday, Christopher Burnes. [*AO*]

28 January 1630
[*see* no. 128]

1 February 1630
[*see* no. 72]

4 February 1630
369 Robert Barnes, S.T.B., rector of East Ilsley, Berks. *Inst.* (f. 26) on the death of Richard Whitwick; patron, Edward Dunch. *Comp.* (334/17 f. 213) 23 Feb. 1630; sureties, Edward Stevens, John Holt. [*AO*]

21 February 1630
370 David Mercer, B.A. (Magdalen, Oxf.), ordained deacon. [*AO*]
[*and see* nos. 347, 363, 367]

24 February 1630
371 Samuel (William) Lloyd, M.A., vicar of Steventon, Berks. *Inst.* (f. 26) on the resignation of William Dillon; patron, John, bishop of Lincoln. [*AO*]
[*and see* no. 113]

25 November 1630[2]
372 Francis Whichelo (Whicheloe), licensed to teach boys at Wallingford, Berks.

3 March 1630
[*see* no. 245]

18 March 1630
373 Richard Steward, LL.D., prebendary of Alton Borealis, vicar of Aldbourne, and rector of Mildenhall. *Inst.* (f. 27) to the prebend and vicarage on the death of John Linch; patron, the bishop; to the rectory on the translation of Walter, bishop of Rochester; patron, the Crown. *Comp.* (334/17 f. 215) 23 Apr. 1630; sureties, John Steward, Anthony Paule. [*AO, FS, PR, WR* p. 10, *DNB*]

20 March 1630
374 Edmund Mason, S.T.P., chaplain to King Charles,[3] dean of Salisbury. *Inst.* (f. 27) on the translation of John Bowle. *Comp.* (334/17 f. 235) 26 Nov. 1630; sureties, Thomas Mason, Henry Calcott. [*AO, FS*]

---

[1] Blewbury was a peculiar of the dean of Salisbury before whom Sampson subscribed 30 Oct. 1629.
[2] Whichelo's subscription, the only one of a schoolmaster in the bishops' book, stands out of chronological sequence on a folio otherwise blank. It is possible that the folio was left blank for a general attempt to collect schoolmasters' subscriptions not proceeded with
[3] See p. 13, n. 1.

25 March 1630
375 John Millett, B.A., licensed to preach at St. Mary's, Wallingford, Berks. [*AO, Conc. Test.*]

6 April 1630
376 John Stubbs, B.A., vicar of Hannington. *Inst.* (f. 27) on the resignation of William Combe; patron, Richard Swayne. [*AO, Conc. Test., FS, PR*]

26 April 1630
377 George Herbert, M.A., rector of Fugglestone and Bemerton.[1] *Inst.* (f. 27) on a translation; patron, the Crown. *Comp.* (334/17 f. 224) 14 July 1630; sureties, George Hulbert, Arthur Wodnoth.

19 September 1630: ordained priest. [*AC, DNB, PR*]

4 May 1630
378 Silvester Goter (Gater, Gother), M.A., vicar of Whiteparish. *Inst.* (f. 27) on the cession of William Parke; patron, John Poucherdon. *Comp.* (334/17 f. 230) 5 Nov. 1630; sureties, John Cobb, James Parry. [*ACO, PR*]
379 John Diment, licensed to preach in the diocese.

20 May 1630
380 Roger Balls, S.T.P., canon of Lyme and Halstock. No subscription.[2] *Inst.* (f. 27) on the translation of Walter Curle as bishop of Bath and Wells. [*AC*]

23 May 1630
381 Robert Tounson, M.A., Fellow of Queens', Camb., ordained priest.

6 June 1632: prebendary of Highworth. *Inst.* (f. 30) on the death of Thomas Fuller; patron, the bishop. *Comp.* (334/18 f. 66) 2 Nov. 1632; sureties, Maurice Henchman, Thomas Merton.

9 April 1633: rector of West Kington. *Inst.* (f. 31) on the death of Benjamin Russel; patron, the bishop. *Comp.* (334/18 f. 85) 24 May 1633; sureties, John Sutton, William Gibbons. [*AC, DNB* (s.v. Robert Townson, bishop of Salisbury), *FS*]
382 Nathaniel Bostocke, M.A., Fellow of Brasenose, Oxf., ordained priest. [*AO*]
383 Constantius Aessop, B.A. (Trinity, Dublin),[3] ordained deacon.

26 February 1632: curate of Collingbourne Ducis, ordained priest.
384 Edmund Parsons, B.A. (Queens', Camb.), curate of Collingbourne Kingston, ordained deacon.

19 December 1630: ordained priest. [*AC*]
385 James Hopkins, B.A. (Exeter, Oxf.), curate of Barford St. Martin, ordained deacon.

26 February 1632: ordained priest. [*AO*]
386 Wolstan Miller, B.A. (Magdalen, Oxf.), curate of Little Langford, ordained deacon. [*AO, WR* p. 377]
387 William Poore, B.A. (Hart Hall, Oxf.), ordained deacon.

[1] See p. 15, n. 3.   [2] It is not clear why Balls's subscription is not recorded. Cf. no. 433.
[3] Aessop is the only subscribing ordinand known to have graduated in Ireland.

22 December 1633: curate of Winterslow, ordained priest. [*AO*]
388 George Foster, *litteratus*, curate of Wittenham Abbas, Berks., ordained deacon.
389 William Bayly, M.A., curate of Swalcliffe, Oxon., ordained priest. [*AO, CR* p. 40]
[*and see* no. 330]

26 May 1630
390 William Buckner, M.A., vicar of Damerham and Martin.[1] *Inst.* (f. 27) on a death; patron, William, earl of Salisbury. *Comp.* (334/17 f. 233) 20 Nov. 1630; sureties, John Meeth, Christopher Brunell.
    5 May 1640: prebendary of Swallowcliffe. No subscription or institution.[2] *Comp.* (334/20 f. 52); sureties, Hugh Welles, John Welles. [*AO, FS, PR, WR*]

12 June 1630
391 Robert Cottesford, M.A., rector of Englefield, Berks. *Inst.* (f. 27) on the death of William Sherington; patron, Ferdinando, Lord Hastings. *Comp.* (334/18 f. 34) 24 Nov. 1631; sureties, Adam Torlesse, Thomas Walker. [*AO, WR* pp. 331–2]

5 July 1630
392 John Mason, B.A., vicar of Faringdon, Berks. No subscription or institution.[3] *Comp.* (334/17 f. 223); sureties, Owen Arthur, John Batling. [? *AC*]

28 July 1630
393 Aylmer Lynch, M.A., licensed to preach in the diocese. [*AC, FS, WR* pp. 376–7]

3 August 1630
394 Francis Dewy, S.T.B., vicar of Chippenham. *Inst.* (f. 27) on the death of William Proudlove; patrons, the dean and chapter of Christ Church, Oxford. *Comp.* (334/17 f. 225) 18 Aug. 1630; sureties, Henry Hunt, Thomas Crasse.
    13 February 1635: rector of Hardenhuish. *Inst.* (f. 34) on the death of Thomas Bridges; patron, Thomas Hawkins. [*AO, PR*]

19 September 1630
395 William Warren, B.A. (Lincoln, Oxf.), ordained deacon.
    25 September 1631: ordained priest. [*AO*]
396 Robert Davenant, M.A., Fellow of St. John's, Oxf., ordained priest.
    16 October 1633:[4] rector of West Kington. *Inst.* (f. 32) on the death of Robert Tounson; patron, the bishop. *Comp.* (334/18 f. 113) 16 Apr. 1634; sureties, Andrew Burton, William Whitby. [*AO, WR*]
397 John Allambridge (Allambrigg, Allainbridge), *litteratus* (Trinity, Camb.),

---

[1] Martin was a chapelry of Damerham: Hoare, *Mod. Wilts.* S. Damerham, 12–18.
[2] Swallowcliffe, a prebend of Heytesbury, was under the jurisdiction of the dean, before whom Buckner subscribed 7 Feb. 1640.
[3] Faringdon was a peculiar of the prebendary of Faringdon. Mason subscribed before the dean 25 June 1630.
[4] See no. 514 and n.

ordained deacon.

23 December 1638: B.A., curate of Edington, ordained priest.

24 December 1638: licensed to preach at Edington and in the diocese. [*AC, WR* p. 380]

398 Richard Spratt, B.A. (St. Edmund Hall, Oxf.), ordained deacon.

23 September 1632: ordained priest. [*AO*]

399 Henry Beach, B.A. (St. Alban Hall, Oxf.), ordained deacon.

24 December 1637: vicar of Coombe Bissett, ordained priest. [*AO, WR*]

400 Richard Pownell (Pembroke, Oxf.),[1] ordained priest. [*AO*]

401 Thomas Simpson, B.A. (Lincoln, Oxf.), ordained priest. [*AO*]

[*and see* nos. 333, 357, 377]

20 October 1630

402 Robert Dyer, M.A., licensed to preach in the diocese.

10 April 1634: rector of Sherrington. No subscription or institution.[2] *Comp.* (334/18 f. 112); sureties, Edward Northey, William Thurman. [*AO, Conc. Test.*]

23 October 1630

403 John Cleaveley, M.A., rector of Beechingstoke. *Inst.* (f. 28) on the death of William Aust; patron, Sir William Button. *Comp.* (334/17 f. 231) 11 Nov. 1630; sureties, Stephen White, John Lowe. [*AO, PR, WR*]

26 October 1630

[*see* no. 342]

3 November 1630

404 William Barlow (Barlowe), S.T.B., rector of West Grimstead. *Inst.* (f. 28) on the death of Edward Hyde; patron, Henry Compton. *Comp.* (334/17 f. 232) 17 Nov. 1630; sureties, John Duke, John Polden. [*AO, PR*][3]

10 November 1630

405 Nicholas Profit (Proffette), M.A., rector of St. Peter's, Marlborough. *Inst.* (f. 28) on the death of Arthur Herne; patron, the bishop. *Comp.* (334/17 f. 235) 26 Nov. 1630; sureties, John Glover, Thomas Nelson. [*ACO, PR*]

4 December 1630

[*see* no. 46]

6 December 1630

[*see* no. 366]

16 December 1630

406 Henry Becke, M.A., rector of Pusey, Berks. *Inst.* (f. 28) on the resignation of Bartholomew Shapley; patron, the bishop. *Comp.* (334/18 f. 1) 4 Jan. 1631; sureties, Gabriel Becke, William Box. [*AO*]

---

[1] Pownell matriculated but apparently did not graduate: *AO*.

[2] For no obvious reason. Sherrington was under the bishop's ordinary jurisdiction.

[3] Barlow was possibly the son of William Barlow (d. 1625), archdeacon of Salisbury, for whom see *D.N.B.*

19 December 1630
407 Henry Craford, B.A. (St. Benedict's,[1] Camb.), ordained deacon.
5 June 1631: curate of Upway, Dors., ordained priest.
408 Nicholas Andrewes, M.A. (Pembroke, Camb.), ordained priest.
14 June 1632: prebendary cf Ilfracombe. *Inst.* (f. 30) on the resignation of Edward Davenant; patron, the bishop. [*AC, FS, WR* pp. 348–9] [*and see* nos. 365, 384]

30 December 1630
409 Leonard Dickenson, M.A., vicar of South Newton. *Inst.* (f. 28) on the death of Thomas Cado; patron, Philip, earl of Pembroke and Montgomery. *Comp.* (334/18 f. 5) 15 Feb. 1631; sureties, John Hollowey, William Coles. [*AC, PR*]

26 January 1631
[*see* no. 127]

6 March 1631
410 Walter Willer, B.A. (Magdalen, Oxf.), ordained priest. [*AO* (Willarde)]
411 Timothy White, B.A. (Clare, Camb.), ordained priest.
22 July 1631: licensed to preach in the diocese. [*AC*]
412 Joseph Tomes, B.A. (Balliol, Oxf.), ordained priest. [*AO*]
413 Thomas Forde, M.A. (Magdalen, Oxf.), ordained deacon. [*AO, DNB*]
414 Robert Clarke (Pembroke, Oxf.),[2] ordained deacon. [? *AO, WR* pp. 180–1]

15 March 1631
[*see* no. 226]

15 April 1631
415 David Stokes, S.T.P., rector of Binfield, Berks. *Inst.* (f. 28) 5 Apr. 1631 on a death; patron, the Crown. *Comp.* (334/18 f. 21) 1 July 1631; sureties, John Tompson, Francis Thrale. [*AO, DNB, WR* p. 380]

30 April 1631
416 Roger Percivall, M.A., licensed to preach at Wilsford and in the diocese.
417 Thomas Watts, M.A., licensed to preach at Speen, Berks., and in the diocese. [? *ACO*]
418 George Wightwicke licenced to preach at East Ilsley, Berks., and in diocese. [*AO*][3]
419 Robert Hawkins, M.A., licensed to preach in the diocese. [*AO, FS*]

2 May 1631
420 James Wilkinson, M.A., licensed to preach in the diocese.
9 February 1636: vicar of Denchworth, Berks. *Inst.* (f. 37); patrons, E. Dover, William Cockayne, Matthew Cradock, and James Price.[4] [*AC*]

---

[1] Otherwise Corpus Christi College.
[2] Clarke's degree, if any, is not known.
[3] Wightwicke was a non-graduate in 1631.
[4] The patrons were possibly trustees of Charles Cockayne, created Viscount Cullen 1642, whose father William had bought the advowson in 1617: *V.C.H. Berks.* iv. 281.

421 Richard Rawling, M.A., licensed to preach in the diocese.

22 May 1633: rector of St. Mary's, Wallingford, Berks. *Inst.* (f. 31); patron, the Crown. [*AO, DNB, WR*]

4 May 1621

422 Robert Symson, M.A., licensed to preach in the diocese. [*AC*]

423 Samuel Clerke, B.A., licensed to preach in the diocese. [*AC*]

10 May 1631

424 John Rand (Rande), B.A., rector of Draycot Cerne. *Inst.* (f. 28) on the resignation of Henry Hunt; patron, Robert Long. [*AC, PR* (Raude), *WR*]

13 May 1631

425 John Berjew, M.A., licensed to preach in the diocese.

18 October 1638: vicar of Norton Bavant. *Inst.* (f. 44); patron, the Crown. [*AO*][1]

20 May 1631

426 James Wedderburne, S.T.P., rector of Patney. *Inst.* (f. 28) on a death; patron, the bishop of Winchester. *Comp.* (334/18 f. 26) 5 Oct. 1631; sureties, Aaron Wilson, George Morris. [*AC, DNB, PR*]

5 June 1631

427 Robert Dove, M.A. (Magdalen, Oxf.), ordained priest. [*AO, WR* p. 79]

428 Hugh Bennett, B.A. (Oriel, Oxf.), ordained deacon.

22 February 1635: curate of Broughton Gifford, ordained priest.[2] [*AO*]

429 Richard Randall, B.A. (Hart Hall, Oxf.), curate of Staverton [Trowbridge parish], ordained deacon.

23 September 1632: ordained priest. [*AO*]

430 John Note, B.A. (Exeter, Oxf.), curate of Little Langford, ordained deacon.

26 February 1632: ordained priest. [*AO, WR* p. 188]

431 Nicholas Gawayne (Gawen), B.A. (Magdalen, Oxf.), curate of Fisherton Anger, ordained deacon.

23 December 1632: ordained priest. [*AO*]

432 Thomas Langrishe, B.A. (Magdalen, Oxf.), curate of Priors Dean, Hants, ordained deacon. [*AO*]

[*and see* nos. 366, 407]

8 June 1631

433 Roger Bates, prebendary of Lyme and Halstock. No subscription or institution.[3] *Comp.* (334/18 f. 18); sureties, John Gibbons, William Parr. [*FS*]

---

[1] Berjew was approved as a preacher by the Long Parliament in 1642: *V.C.H. Wilts.* viii. 56.

[2] A note in the subscription book reads: 'Let enquiry be made concerning Hugh Bennett'. It possibly refers to his letters testimonial.

[3] It is not clear why Bates's subscription is not recorded. Cf. no. 380.

10 June 1631
434 Edmund Holford, M.A. (Corpus Christi, Oxf.), licensed to preach in the diocese. [*AO*]

18 June 1631
[*see* no. 126]

22 June 1631
[*see* no. 191]

23 June 1631
435 Thomas Lushington, S.T.B., prebendary of Beaminster Secunda. *Inst.* (f. 29) on the resignation of Richard, bishop of Oxford; patron, the Crown. *Comp.* (334/18 f. 23) 31 July 1631; sureties, William Lewyn, Sion Hill. [*AO, FS, DNB, WR* p. 270]

29 June 1631
[*see* no. 217]

18 July 1631
436 James Whitney, S.T.B., rector of Donhead St. Andrew. *Inst.* (f. 29) on the death of John Button; patron, Joseph Bower. *Comp.* (334/18 f. 31) 14 Nov. 1631; sureties, John Bateman, Edward Reynolds. [*AO, PR, WR*]

22 July 1631
[*see* no. 411]

30 July 1631
437 Richard Mervyn, M.A., rector of Pertwood. *Inst.* (f. 29) on the death of Arthur Fletcher; patron, Thomas Mervyn. [*AO, PR, WR* pp. 118–19]

25 September 1631
438 William Squire,[1] M.A. (Oxf.),[2] ordained priest. [*AO*]
439 Samuel Tomlins, M.A. (Emmanuel, Camb.), ordained priest. [*AC*]
440 Joseph Newley, M.A. (Magdalen, Oxf.), ordained priest.
441 John Eastgate, B.A. (Exeter and St. Mary Hall, Oxf.), curate of Berwick St. John, ordained deacon.
   21 December 1634: curate of Fonthill Bishop, ordained priest. [*AO*]
442 George (Edward) Jenkins, B.A. (St. Mary Hall, Oxf.), curate of Sedgehill, ordained deacon.
   23 September 1632: ordained priest. [*AO, Conc. Test.*]
443 Edward Pilsworth, B.A. (Magdalen, Oxf.), curate of Corsham, ordained deacon.
   13 March 1636: curate of Winterbourne Bassett, ordained priest. [*AO*]
444 William Reeve, B.A. (Pembroke, Oxf.), curate of Wickham [Welford parish], Berks., ordained deacon.
   17 March 1633: ordained priest.
[*and see* no. 395]

[1] Cf. no. 227. It is possible but, because of the 6-year interval between deaconing and priesting, not likely that nos. 227 and 438 concern the same man.
[2] The college is not named.

27 September 1631
445 John Harding, M.A., vicar of Ashbury, Berks. *Inst.* (f. 29) on the resignation of Francis White; patron, Sir Henry Martin. *Comp.* (334/18 f. 50) 9 May 1632; sureties, John Doyly, Stephen Baron. [*AO, CR* p. 247]

12 October 1631
446 Robert Anton, M.A., vicar of Stratfield Mortimer, Berks. *Inst.* (f. 29) on the death of David George; patron, Eton College. [*AC*]

10 October 1631 [1]
447 Nicholas Tackle, licensed to preach in the diocese.

3 December 1631
448 Henry Braie (Bray), M.A., rector of Foxley. *Inst.* (f. 29) on a death; patron, Sir George Ayliffe. [*AO, PR*]

17 December 1631
449 John Awdry, M.A., curate of Melksham, ordained priest.
450 William Woodward, B.A., curate of North Waltham, Hants, ordained priest. [*AO, WR* pp. 300, 377]
451 John Hardwicke, B.A., curate of Donhead St. Andrew, ordained priest. [*AO*]

18 December 1631
452 Francis Peckston, B.A., curate of Pewsey, ordained priest. [*AO* (Pexton)]
453 John Myhell, B.A. (Oriel, Oxf.), curate of Bridport, Dors., ordained deacon. [*AO*]
454 John Hayne, B.A. (Trinity, Oxf), curate of West Lulworth, Dors., ordained deacon. [*AO, WR*]
[*and see* no. 297]

19 January 1632
[*see* no. 101]

7 February 1632
455 Humphrey Newbury,[2] B.A., vicar of Waltham St. Lawrence, Berks. *Inst.* (f. 29); patron, the Crown. [*AO*]

13 February 1632
[*see* no. 321]

14 February 1631
456 Nathaniel Field, M.A., rector of Stourton. *Inst.* (f. 29); patron, John Kinge. *Comp.* (334/18 f. 44) 12 Mar. 1632; sureties, Josiah Harris, Edward Harris. [*PR, WR*]

---

[1] This subscription stands out of chronological order for no obvious reason.
[2] Cf. no. 329. In 1632 the Crown presented because of the minority of Richard Neville: *V.C.H. Berks.* iii. 184. The Humphrey Newbury instituted in 1629 was possibly not the Humphrey Newbury instituted in 1632 since there is no apparent reason for a representation.

26 February 1632
457 Francis Frampton, B.A. (St. Mary Hall, Oxf.), curate of Holme Priory [East Holme parish], Dors., ordained priest. [*AO*]
458 Benjamin Walter, B.A. (Magdalen, Oxf.), curate of Horningsham, ordained deacon. [*AO*]
459 John Fyler, B.A. (Balliol, Oxf.), curate of Cranborne, Dors., ordained deacon. [*AO*]
460 John Phipp, B.A. (Magdalen, Oxf.), ordained deacon.
    7 March 1639: rector of Teffont Evias. *Inst.* (f. 46) on the death of Gabriel Lastyate; patron, Nicholas Phipp. *Comp.* (334/20 f. 54) 15 May 1640; sureties, William Wheeler, Thomas Baker. [*AO, CR*]
461 John Clark, M.A. (Jesus, Camb.), curate of Cheriton, Hants, ordained priest. [*AC*]
[*and see* nos. 383, 385, 430]

3 March 1632
[*see* no. 268]

28 March 1632
[*see* no. 340]

25 May 1632
462 Richard Bristow (Bristowe), M.A., rector of Didcot, Berks. *Inst.* (f. 29) on the death of John Seller; patron, Henry Bristow. *Comp.* (334/18 f. 64) 22 Oct. 1632; sureties, Thomas Cotchet, Thomas Matthew.
    7 October 1637: vicar of East Hagbourne, Berks. *Inst.* (f. 42) on the death of Laurence Wright; patron, John Bristowe. *Comp.* (334/18 f. 212) 19 Oct. 1637; sureties, Thomas Laxton, George Godfrey. [*AO*]

6 June 1632
[*see* nos. 299, 381]

14 June 1632
[*see* nos. 127, 408]

22 June 1632
[*see* no. 255]

8 August 1632
463 Robert Thompson, M.A., rector of Broughton Gifford. *Inst.* (f. 30) on a cession; patron, the Crown. [*AC, PR*]

29 August 1632
464 William Lyford, S.T.B., rector of Peasemore, Berks. *Inst.* (f. 30) 19 Aug. 1632 on the death of William Lyford; patron, Edward Pococke. *Comp.* (334/18 f. 64) 8 Oct. 1632; sureties, Gilbert Harrison, John Pococke. [*AO*]

23 September 1632[1]
465 Edward Fauconer (Falconer), B.A. (Magdalen, Oxf.), ordained deacon.
    22 December 1633: vicar of Britford, ordained priest. *Comp.* (334/18 f. 124] 4 July 1634; sureties, John Chappell, Charles Powell. [*AO, CR, Conc. Test.*)

[1] See below nos. 470–4 and n. 4.

24 September 1632
466 Gilbert Talbot,[1] M.A., rector of Liddington.[2] *Inst.* (f. 30) on the death of Nathaniel Torperley; patron, Sir John St. John. *Comp.* (334/18 f. 79) 13 Mar. 1633; sureties, Gilbert Sheldon, Richard Ottoley.
    29 November 1633: prebendary of Liddington. [*PR*]

10 October 1632
467 Thomas Lockey, M.A., vicar of East Garston, Berks. *Inst.* (f. 30); patrons, the dean and chapter of Christ Church, Oxford. *Comp.* (334/18 f. 66) 6 Nov. 1632; sureties, Thomas Anston, Henry Savage. [*AO, DNB*]

13 December 1632
468 John Carse, S.T.P., rector of Brixton Deverill. *Inst.* (f. 30) on the translation of Robert, bishop of Bristol; patron, the Crown. *Comp.* (334/18 f. 74) 9 Jan. 1633; sureties, William Penycooke, Robert Huiheson.
    18 May 1637: rector of Hamstead Marshall, Berks. *Inst.* (f. 40) on the death of Richard Ridley; patron, William, Lord Craven.
    19 May 1637: prebendary of Bedminster and Ratcliffe. *Inst.* (f. 40) on the death of Giles Thornburgh; patron, the bishop. *Comp.* (334/18 f. 205) for the rectory and the prebend 8 June 1637; sureties, Robert Hutchinson, John Colvill. [*AC, FS, PR, WR*]

14 December 1632
[*see* no. 44]

23 December 1632[3]
469 Leonard Alexander, LL.B. (New, Oxf.), ordained priest. [*AO, WR* p. 369]

23 September 1632[4]
470 Matthew Buckett, B.A., ordained priest. [*AO, PR*][5]
471 Gilbert Talbot[6] (All Souls', Oxf.),[7] ordained deacon.
    29 November 1633: rector of Liddington.[8] *Inst.* (f. 32) on the resignation of Gilbert Talbot; patron, Sherington Talbot. *Comp.* (334/18 f. 116) 6 May 1634; sureties, Gilbert Sheldon, John Willis.
472 Robert Harris, M.A. (Magdalen, Oxf.), ordained priest. [*AO, PR*]
473 Christopher Foull (Fole), B.A. (Magdalen, Oxf.), ordained deacon.
    16 June 1633: ordained priest.
    20 January 1635: vicar of Stratton St. Margaret. *Inst.* (f. 33) on the cession of Walter Attwood; patron, Merton College, Oxford. [*AO* (Fowle)]

1 The elder Gilbert Talbot: cf. no. 471.
2 The rectory or prebend was a sinecure: *V.C.H. Wilts.* ix. 72. Cf. no. 471.
3 See below n. 4 and nos. 475–82.
4 The Michaelmas ordination subscriptions for 1632 begin a new page of the book leaving a space after the subscription for institution (no. 465). That space was filled by nos. 466–9. Leonard Alexander's subscription (no. 469) is on the same page as the Michaelmas subscriptions but, dated 23 Dec., presumably belongs with the Christmas subscriptions.
5 Buckett, as vicar of North Bradley in the Interregnum, resisted the radical tendencies there: *V.C.H. Wilts.* viii. 227–8.
6 The younger Gilbert Talbot: cf. no. 466.
7 Talbot's degree, if any, is not known.
8 Cf. no. 466 and n.

474 Thomas Coles, M.A. (Balliol, Oxf.), ordained deacon.

6 July 1633: prebendary of Hill Deverill. No subscription or institution.[1]
Comp. (334/18 f. 91); surety, William Coles.

18 August 1636: rector of Fifield Bavant. *Inst.* (f. 38) on the death of
Thomas Coles; patrons, Roger Coles and William Coles. *Comp.* (334/18
f. 191) 7 Feb. 1637; sureties, William Coles, Thomas Carter.

5 March 1637: ordained priest. [*AO*]
[*and see* nos. 398, 429, 442, 465]

14 December 1632
[*see* no. 44]

23 December 1632[2]
475 Richard Eburne, B.A. (Queen's, Oxf.), ordained priest. [*Conc. Test.*]
476 John Talbot, M.A. (St. Alban Hall, Oxf.), ordained priest. [*AO, WR*
p. 137]
477 James Pyke, B.A. (Oriel, Oxf.), ordained priest. [*AO*]
478 Robert Maton, M.A. (Wadham, Oxf.), ordained deacon.

24 May 1635: ordained priest. [*AO* (Roger Maton), *Conc. Test., DNB*]
479 Robert Ward, B.A. (Balliol, Oxf.), ordained deacon. [*AO*]
480 Anthony Stephens, B.A. (St. John's, Oxf.), ordained deacon.

17 March 1633: ordained priest.

18 March 1633: vicar of Swindon.[3] [*AO*]
481 William Ailesbury, B.A. (Christ's, Camb.), ordained deacon. [*AC*]
482 Evan Lloyd, M.A., vicar of Steventon, Berks. *Inst.* (f. 30) on the cession
of Samuel Lloyd; patron, John, bishop of Lincoln. [*AO*]
[*and see* nos. 431, 469]

4 January 1633
483 Edmund Knevett, M.A., rector of East Coulston. *Inst.* (f. 30) on a
cession; patron, the Crown. [*AO, PR, WR*]

4 February 1633
see no. 172]

9 February 1633
[*see* no. 307]

27 February 1633
[*see* no. 287]

29 February 1633
484 Richard Zsouche (Zouch), LL.D., Regius Professor of Civil Law

---

[1] The prebend was under the jurisdiction of the dean before whom Coles subscribed
30 Nov. 1632.
[2] See above p. 56, n. 4.
[3] Stephens's subscription as vicar of Swindon, where William Callimore succeeded his
father William as vicar in 1634 (nos. 169, 556), was possibly made under a misappre-
hension. There is no record of his institution. He subscribed before the dean as a
schoolmaster of Highworth 29 May 1634.

Oxford, prebendary of Shipton.[1] *Inst.* (f. 31) on the death of George Proctor. [*AO, WR*]

17 March 1633[2]
485 Rhys Tynte, M.A. (Balliol, Oxf.), ordained deacon. [*AO*]
486 John Trotte, ordained priest.
487 Samuel Forward, B.A. (Trinity, Oxf.), ordained priest. [*AO, WR* p. 373]
488 William Benet (Bennett), *alumnus* of Hart Hall, Oxf., curate of Maddington, ordained deacon.
22 December 1633: ordained priest. [? *AO*]
489 Caleb Tucker, B.A. (New Inn Hall, Oxf.), ordained deacon. [*AO*]

16 March 1633
490 Thomas Lawrence, S.T.B., rector of Fugglestone and Bemerton.[3] *Inst.* (f. 31) on the death of George Herbert; patron, Philip, earl of Pembroke. *Comp.* (334/18 f. 82) 3 May 1633; sureties, Gilbert Sheldon, John Willis. [*ACO, PR, WR*]

17 March 1633[4]
491 Henry Rogers, B.A. (Lincoln, Oxf.), ordained priest.
7 January 1636: licensed to preach in the diocese. [*AO*]
492 John West, B.A. (Trinity, Camb.), ordained priest. [*AC, WR*]
493 Robert Hall, LL.B. (New, Oxf.), ordained deacon. [*AO*]
[*and see* nos. 444, 480]

18 March 1633
[*see* no. 480]

9 April 1633
[*see* no. 381]

15 May 1633
494 Peter Gibson, M.A., vicar of Sonning, Berks. No subscription or institution.[5] *Comp.* (334/18 f. 83); sureties, James Gibson, Francis Dere. [*AO*]

22 May 1633
[*see* no. 421]

28 May 1633
495 Henry Scudder, M.A., rector of Collingbourne Ducis. *Inst.* (f. 31); patron, the Crown. *Comp.* (334/18 f. 91) 3 July 1633; sureties, William Bisby, Edward Miller. [*AC, DNB, PR*]

1 The stall and chair were linked and the prebend could be held by a layman, which Zsouche was: *V.C.H. Wilts.* iii. 191.
2 And see nos. 491–3.
3 Lawrence's subscription was dated 16 Mar. It stands at the bottom of a page and was possibly entered before those of the ordinands. It is also possible, but less likely, that 16 Mar. was a mistake for 17 Mar. Bemerton was a chapelry of Fugglestone: no. 38 n.
4 And see nos. 485–9.
5 Sonning was a peculiar of the dean before whom Gibson subscribed 14 May 1633.

496 Charles Robson, M.A., prebendary of Stratford. *Inst.* (f. 31) on the death of Benjamin Russel; patron, the bishop. [*AO, DNB, FS*]

16 June 1633
497 Alexander Randall, B.A. (Lincoln, Oxf.), ordained deacon.
    18 February 1638: curate of Bradford on Avon, ordained priest. [*WR* p. 318]
498 Anthony Hawles, M.A. (Queen's, Oxf.), ordained deacon.
    4 June 1637: ordained priest. [*AO, FS, PR, WR* p. 14]
499 George Lovell, M.A. (Hart Hall, Oxf.), ordained priest. [*AO*]
500 William Dringe, M.A. (Queen's, Oxf.), ordained deacon. [*AO*]
501 John Stephens, M.A. (St. Mary Hall, Oxf.), ordained deacon. [? *AO*]
502 Robert Sawer, B.A. (Queen's, Oxf.), ordained deacon. [*AO* (Sayer), *WR* p. 29]
[*and see* no. 473]

20 June 1633
503 Christopher Ryly (Ryley), S.T.B., rector of Newton Tony. *Inst.* (f. 31) on the death of Fortunate Saunders; patron, Francis Jones. *Comp.* (334/18 f. 98) 28 Oct. 1633; sureties, Owen Champneys, Robert Feltham. [*AO, PR, WR*]

3 July 1633
[*see* no. 307]

6 July 1633
[*see* no. 474]

7 July 1633
[*see* no. 344]

12 July 1633
504 Richard Nixon, M.A., vicar of Chaddleworth, Berks. *Inst.* (f. 31) on a death; patron, John, bishop of Lincoln.
    14 November 1637: vicar of Chieveley, Berks. *Inst.* (f. 42) on the death of Edward Pococke; patron, Richard Pococke. *Comp.* (334/18 f. 218) 24 Nov. 1637; sureties, John Barkesdale, Bernard Lyford. [*AO, WR*]

15 July 1633
505 Edmund Proby, M.A., rector of Broughton Gifford. *Inst.* (f. 31) on a resignation; patron, the Crown. *Comp.* (334/18 f. 102) 22 Nov. 1633; sureties, Humphrey Proby, Emanuel Proby.
    22 September 1634: licensed to preach in the diocese. [*AC, PR, WR*]

19 July 1633
506 William Cosyn, M.A., vicar of Shinfield with Swallowfield, Berks.[1] *Inst.* (f. 31) on the death of Thomas Flasket; patron, the dean of Hereford. *Comp.* (334/18 f. 95) 29 Aug. 1633; sureties, Richard Wormsall, Edward Cozins. [*AC*]

---

[1] Swallowfield was a chapelry of Shinfield: *V.C.H. Berks.* iii. 273–4.

24 July 1633
507 George Russel (Russell), vicar of Littleton Drew.[1] *Inst.* (f. 31) on the death of Benjamin Russel; patron, the bishop.
   2 March 1634: ordained priest. [*PR*]

13 August 1633
508 Ralph Boden, M.A., vicar of Aldermaston, Berks. *Inst.* (f. 31) on the cession of Stephen Rose; patron, Sir Humphrey Forster. *Comp.* (334/18 f. 98) 19 Oct. 1633; sureties, John Bimbury, Matthew Smith. [*AO*]

15 August 1633
509 Henry Hammond (Hamandus), B.A., licensed to preach at All Cannings and Etchilhampton.[2] [*ACO*]

28 September 1633
510 David (Daniel) Letsham, rector of St. Peter's, Wallingford, Berks. *Inst.* (f. 31) on the resignation of Edmund Truelocke; patron, John Gregory.
511 Hugh Halswell, M.A., rector of Codford St. Peter. *Inst.* (f. 32) on the death of Christopher Dugdale; patron, Philip, earl of Pembroke. *Comp.* (334/18 f. 98) 19 Oct. 1633; sureties, Henry Halswell, Charles Coventry. [*AO, PR, WR* p. 184]

1 October 1633
512 Christopher Tesdale, M.A., rector of Rollestone. *Inst.* (f. 32) on a death; patron, the Crown. *Comp.* (334/18 f. 98) 19 Oct. 1633; sureties, Edward Palmer, Anthony Wright. [*AO, PR, WR* p. 380]

2 October 1633
513 John Head, M.A., rector of Catmore, Berks. *Inst.* (f. 32) on the death of Stephen Stampe; patron, Richard Yate. [*AO*]

16 October 1633
514 John Tounson, M.A., prebendary of Highworth. *Inst.* (f. 32) on the death of Robert Tounson; patron, the bishop.[3] *Comp.* (334/18 f. 136) 28 Nov. 1633; sureties, Edward Henchman, Maurice Henchman.
   21 September 1634: ordained priest.
   24 May 1639: vicar of Bremhill. *Inst.* (f. 47) on the death of Thomas Collyer; patron, the bishop. *Comp.* (334/20 f. 29) 4 Sept. 1639; sureties, James Medlicott, William Sompner. [*AO, DNB* (s.v. Robert Townson, bishop of Salisbury)]
[*and see* no. 396]

31 October 1633
515 Richard Edmondson, S.T.B., vicar of Sparsholt, Berks. *Inst.* (f. 32) on

---

[1] Littleton Drew was subsequently a rectory: *Returns to Visitation Queries 1783*, ed. Mary Ransome (W.R.S. xxvii), p. 36 n.
[2] Etchilhampton was a chapelry of All Cannings: *V.C.H. Wilts.* x. 30.
[3] Robert Tounson was succeeded as prebendary by his brother John on the day that his cousin Robert Davenant succeeded him as rector of West Kington (no. 396). All three were nephews of Bishop Davenant.

the death of John Williamson; patron, Queen's College, Oxford. *Comp.* (334/18 f. 99) 11 Nov. 1633; sureties, Humphrey Robinson, Nicholas Longe. [*AO*]

13 November 1633
516 Thomas Drope, S.T.B., vicar of Cumnor, Berks. *Inst.* (f. 32) on the death of Thomas Drope; patrons, John Peacocke and Robert Phillipson. *Comp.* (334/18 f. 104) 28 Nov. 1633; sureties, John Peacocke, William Sems. [*AO, DNB* (s.v. Francis Drope)]

29 November 1633
[*see* nos. 466, 471]

4 December 1633
517 John (Joseph) Cleaver, M.A., vicar of New Windsor, Berks. *Inst.* (f. 32) on a death; patron, the Crown. *Comp.* (334/18 f. 113) 23 Apr. 1634; sureties, Francis Cleaver, Henry Cleaver. [*AO*]

21 December 1633
518 Thomas Robinson *alias* Hunt, [M.A.,] licensed to preach at Lacock. [*AO*]

22 December 1633
519 Theophilus Powell, M.A. (Christ Church, Oxf.), ordained deacon. [*AO, ? WR* p. 121]
520 James Masters, M.A. (St. Alban Hall, Oxf.), domestic chaplain to John Popham of Littlecote,[1] ordained priest. [*AO, WR* p. 316]
521 Ralph Adames, M.A. (Magdalen, Oxf.), curate of Cholsey, Berks. [*AO*]
522 John Langton, M.A. (Magdalen, Oxf.), ordained deacon.
21 September 1634: rector of Great Somerford, ordained priest. *Comp.* (334/18 f. 118) 20 May 1634; sureties, Edward Hilliard, Richard Gerard. [*AO*]
523 Nathaniel Eaton, M.A. (Trinity, Camb.), curate of Dinton, ordained deacon. [*AC, DNB*]
524 William Lockey, B.A. (New Inn Hall, Oxf.), curate of Kingston Lisle, Berks., ordained priest. [*AO*]
525 Walter Rosewell, M.A. (Magdalen, Oxf.), curate of Newbury, Berks., ordained priest. [*ACO, CR* pp. 418–19]
526 William Toomer, B.A. (Magdalen, Oxf.), curate of Semley, ordained deacon.
21 December 1634: curate of Bemerton [Fugglestone parish], ordained priest. [*AO, CR* p. 489]
527 William Skinner, B.A. (New Inn Hall, Oxf.), curate of Sutton Courtenay, Berks., ordained deacon. [*AO*]
528 Thomas Codrington, B.A. (St. Alban Hall, Oxf.), curate of Dodington, Glos., ordained deacon. [*AO*]

---

1 Masters's is the only subscription of a domestic chaplain recorded in the bishops' book.

529 Benjamin Hancock, B.A. (St. John's, Oxf.), curate of Romsey, Hants, ordained deacon. [*AO*]

530 William Hart, B.A. (New Inn Hall, Oxf.), curate of Ogbourne St. Andrew, ordained deacon. [*AO, PR*]

531 Richard Claycott, M.A. (Trinity, Oxf.), curate of Donhead St. Andrew, ordained deacon.

532 George Mundey, B.A. (Pembroke, Oxf.), curate of Freefolk [Whitchurch parish, Hants], Winchester diocese, ordained deacon. [*AO*]

533 Thomas Butler, M.A. (Wadham, Oxf.), curate of Hilton, [Dors.,] Bristol diocese, ordained deacon.

    1 June 1634: ordained priest. [*AO*]

534 Samuel Edwards, B.A. (New Inn Hall, Oxf.), curate of Shroton, [Dors.,] Bristol diocese, ordained deacon. [*AO*]

535 Robert Ryves, LL.B., Fellow of New, Oxf., ordained priest. [*AO*]
[*and see* nos. 335, 387, 465, 488]

8 January 1634
[*see* nos. 179, 255]

7 February 1634
536 Francis Price, M.A., vicar of East Garston, Berks. *Inst.* (f. 32) on the resignation of Thomas Lockey; patrons, the dean and chapter of Christ Church, Oxford. *Comp.* (334/18 f. 112) 29 Mar. 1634; sureties, William Sorrel, John Crismond. [*AO*]

2 March 1634
537 Thomas Skinner, M.A. (St. Edmund Hall, Oxf.), ordained priest. [*AO*]
538 Richard Alleine, B.A. (New Inn Hall, Oxf.), ordained priest.
    25 May 1635: licensed to preach in the diocese. [*AO, CR* p. 6, *DNB*]
539 Matthias Davis, B.A. (Christ Church, Oxf.), ordained priest. [*AO*]
540 Thomas Foote, B.A. (Pembroke, Oxf.), ordained deacon.
    25 September 1636: curate of Chilmark, ordained priest. [*AO*]
541 Thomas Worrall, B.A. (Brasenose, Oxf.), ordained deacon. [*AO, WR* p. 72]
[*and see* nos. 277, 507]

10 April 1634
[*see* no. 402]

29 April 1634
[*see* no. 49]

1 June 1634
542 William Swarpbrock, M.A. (St. Mary Hall, Oxf.), ordained deacon.
543 Edward Cornelius, M.A. (Magdalen, Oxf.), ordained priest. [*AO*]
544 Thomas Collinson, B.A. (All Souls', Oxf.), ordained deacon.
    12 June 1636: curate of New Windsor, Berks., ordained priest. [*AO*]
545 John Ferris, B.A., ordained priest.

11 August 1635: curate of Colerne, licensed to preach in the diocese. [*AO, PR*]
[*and see* nos. 346, 533]

17 June 1634
546 Stephen Everard *alias* Webb, rector of Allington. No subscription or institution.[1] *Comp.* (334/18 f. 122); sureties, Stephen Worlidge, Stephen Aylwin. [*AO*]

4 September 1634
547 John Turner, rector of Eaton Hastings, Berks. No subscription or institution.[2] *Comp.* (334/18 f. 127); sureties, Adam Manwaringe, Thomas Pywall. [? *AC*]

18 September 1634
548 Nathaniel Wilkinson, [M.A.,] vicar of Bradford on Avon. *Inst.* (f. 32) on a death; patrons, William Porrett and Edward Craddocke. *Comp.* (334/18 f. 130) 9 Oct. 1634: sureties, William Franklin, John Smith. [*AO, PR, WR* p. 321]

21 September 1634
549 George Bell, B.A. (Merton, Oxf.), ordained priest. [*AO*]
550 Benjamin Gastrell, M.A. (New Inn Hall, Oxf.), ordained deacon. [*AO*]
551 John Antram, M.A. (Hart Hall, Oxf.), ordained deacon.
   20 September 1635: curate of Little Langford, ordained priest. [*AO, WR* p. 127]
552 John Wheller, M.A. (Magdalen, Oxf.), ordained deacon.
   24 May 1635: ordained priest. [*AO* (Wheeler)]
553 Thomas Clethero, B.A. (Christ Church, Oxf.), ordained deacon. [*AO* (Clitherow)]
554 William Aust, B.A. (St. Edmund Hall, Oxf.), ordained deacon.
   23 December 1638: curate of Great Durnford, ordained priest. [*ACO, PR*]
555 Joseph Hill, M.A. (Pembroke, Oxf.), ordained deacon.
   18 August 1637: rector of Hinton Waldrist, Berks. *Inst.* (f. 41) on the cession of Joseph Hill; patron, Sir Henry Marten. *Comp.* (334/18 f. 219) 29 Nov. 1637; sureties, Richard Ferrand, John Watkinson. [*AO, WR*]
[*and see* nos. 514, 522]

22 September 1634
556 William Callimore (Gallimore),[3] M.A., vicar of Swindon, licensed to preach in the diocese.
   29 November 1634: vicar of Swindon. *Inst.* (f. 33) on the resignation of William Callimore; patron, the Crown. *Comp.* (334/18 f. 137) 29 Nov. 1634;

[1] For no obvious reason. Allington was under the bishop's ordinary jurisdiction.
[2] For no obvious reason. Eaton Hastings was under the bishop's ordinary jurisdiction.
[3] Cf. nos. 169, 480 and n. It is not certain whether the licence to preach given 22 Sept. was to the younger or elder William Callimore. It seems likely that a dispute over the vicarage between Anthony Stephens (no. 480) and the younger Callimore following the resignation of the elder Callimore was settled by the Crown's presentation of Callimore, and that it was he who was licensed to preach.

sureties, William Morse, Robert Whippe. [PR]

557 Robert Nicholson, M.A., curate of Purton, licensed to preach in the diocese.

12 March 1638: vicar of Fisherton de la Mere. *Inst.* (f. 42) on the resignation of Samuel Michell; patron, John Froyle. [AO]
[*and see* nos. 259, 505]

2 October 1634
558 Thomas Clerke, M.A., prebendary of Uffculme. *Inst.* (f. 32) on the resignation of Thomas Clarke; patron, the bishop. *Comp.* (334/18 f. 136) 28 Nov. 1634; sureties, Edward Henchman, Maurice Henchman. [? *ACO, FS*]

22 October 1634
559 Richard Jenings (Jennings), rector of Calstone Wellington. *Inst.* (f. 32) on the death of Henry Jennings; patron, John Ducket. [PR]

25 October 1634
560 Thomas Hall, LL.B., vicar of Marcham, Berks. *Inst.* (f. 32) on the resignation of Thomas Westley; patrons, the dean and chapter of Christ Church, Oxford. *Comp.* (334/18 f. 134); sureties, Joseph Dangham, Thomas Tarbecke.

27 October 1634
561 John Osborne, [M.A.,] vicar of Letcombe Regis, Berks. No subscription or institution.[1] *Comp.* (334/18 f. 132); sureties, Edward Osborne, William Osborne. [AO]

18 November 1634
562 Walter Atwood, M.A., vicar of Warminster. *Inst.* (f. 33); patron, the Crown. *Comp.* (334/18 f. 136) 28 Nov. 1634; sureties, John Atwood, William Whitfield.

21 May 1635: licensed to preach in the diocese. [AC, PR]

19 November 1634
563 John Rogers, M.A., prebendary of Chute and Chisenbury. *Inst.* (f. 33) on the cession of Edward Davenant; patron, the bishop. *Comp.* (334/18 f. 136) 26 Nov. 1634; sureties, Henry Clinket, William Tiffin.

25 November 1635: vicar of Warminster. *Inst.* (f. 37) on the death of Walter Atwood. *Comp.* (334/18 f. 167) 23 Dec. 1635; sureties, Richard Clay, William Tiffin.

2 March 1640: vicar of Aldbourne. *Inst.* (f. 48) on the resignation of Richard Steward and (f. 49) 24 Mar. 1640.[2]

24 March 1640: rector of Compton Bassett. *Inst.* (f. 49) on the resignation of Rice Pugh; patron, the bishop. *Comp.* (334/20 f. 49) 15 Apr. 1640; sureties, Thomas Frith, George Clay.

19 August 1640: vicar of Westbury. No subscription or institution.[3] *Comp.* (334/20 f. 63); sureties, Thomas Frith, George Clay. [AO, FS]
[*and see* no. 127]

---

[1] For no obvious reason. Letcombe Regis was under the bishop's ordinary jurisdiction.
[2] See no. 809 and n.
[3] Westbury was a peculiar of the precentor of Salisbury: see no. 165 n.

20 November 1634
[*see* no. 251]

29 November 1634
[*see* no. 556]

6 December 1634
[*see* no. 147]

21 December 1634
564 Philip Kingsman, M.A. (Magdalen, Oxf.), curate of Leigh Delamere, ordained deacon.
   23 December 1634: rector of Leigh Delamere. *Inst.* (f. 33) on the death of Robert Latymer; patron, Henry Chiver.
   20 September 1635: ordained priest. [*AO, PR*]
565 Francis Bellingham, M.A. (New Inn Hall, Oxf.), ordained deacon.
   22 February 1635: ordained priest. [*AO*]
566 William Pitkin, M.A. (Pembroke, Oxf.), curate of Chilton, Berks., ordained deacon. [*AO*]
567 Samuel Ainsworth, B.A. (Oriel, Oxf.), ordained deacon. [*AO, CR* p. 3]
568 Alan Figes (Wadham, Oxf.), curate of Odstock, ordained deacon.
569 Thomas Ladde, B.A. (Hart Hall, Oxf.), curate of Figheldean, ordained deacon.
   24 May 1635: ordained priest.
   17 May 1638: licensed to preach at Compton Bassett. [*AO*]
570 Robert Read, B.A. (St. Edmund Hall, Oxf.), curate of Ardington, Berks., ordained deacon.
   12 June 1636: curate of East Hendred, Berks., ordained priest. [*AO*]
571 Robert Langton, M.A. (Magdalen, Oxf.), curate of Great Somerford, ordained deacon. [*AO*]
572 John Tulse, M.A. (Christ Church, Oxf.), curate of Pimperne, Dors., ordained priest. [*AO*]
[*and see* nos. 441, 526]

23 December 1634
[*see* no. 564]

20 January 1635
[*see* no. 473]

23 January 1635
[*see* no. 335]

5 February 1635
573 John Barnstone, S.T.P., rector of Winterslow. *Inst.* (f. 33) on the death of Nicholas Ely; patron, Alexander Thistlethwait. *Comp.* (334/18 f. 144) 12 Mar. 1635; sureties, Humphrey Cravener, William Taylor. [*AO, DNB, FS, PR, WR* p. 14]

13 February 1635
[*see* no. 394]

22 February 1635
574 John Collier, B.A. (Oriel, Oxf.), ordained deacon.
   23 September 1638: curate of Dunwear,[1] Som., ordained priest. [*AO*]
[*and see* nos. 428, 565]

17 March 1635
575 Richard Smith (Smythe), M.A., vicar of Liddington. *Inst.* (f. 34) on the death of Ellis Edwards; patron, John Smythe. *Comp.* (334/18 f. 149) 14 May 1635; sureties, Robert Whippe, William Morse. [*AO, PR*]

26 March 1635
576 Edward Hutchins, M.A., rector of Easton Grey. *Inst.* (f. 35) on the resignation of William Kenne; patron, Thomas Hodges. [*AO, CR* p. 286, *PR*]

16 April 1635
577 John Newton, M.A. (Brasenose, Oxf.), licensed to preach in the diocese. [*AO, WR*]

22 April 1635
578 Richard Baylie, S.T.P., royal chaplain,[2] dean of Salisbury. *Inst.* (f. 35). *Comp.* (334/18 f. 150) 16 May 1635; sureties, William Torlesse, William Dell.
   10 December 1637: rector of Bradfield, Berks. *Inst.* (f. 42) on the death of John, bishop of Rochester; patron, the Crown. *Comp.* (334/18 f. 228) 30 Mar. 1638; sureties, Adam Torlesse, William Duckett. [*AO, FS, WR*]

25 April 1635
579 Henry Swaddon, M.A., rector of Sutton Veny. *Inst.* (f. 35) on the death of Walter Conningsby; patron, Sir William Button. *Comp.* (334/18 f. 147) 4 May 1635; sureties, George Lowe, William Deane. [*AO, PR, WR*]

4 May 1635
580 Henry Jolly, [M.A.,] vicar of Chute. No subscription or institution.[3] *Comp.* (334/18 f. 147); sureties, William Osborne, Thomas Watts. [*AC*]

5 May 1635
581 William Dickenson, S.T.B., rector of Besselsleigh (Bilesley *alias* Leigh), Berks. *Inst.* (f. 35); patron, William Lenthall.
   18 November 1635: rector of Besselsleigh. *Inst.* (f. 36); patron, the Crown.[4] [*AO, WR*]

21 May 1635
582 John Courtice, B.A., licensed to preach in the diocese. [*AO*]
[*and see* no. 562]

22 May 1635
[*see* no. 99]

---

[1] The reading of the MS., 'Dunwer' or 'Dunna', is not certain.
[2] See no. 3 n.
[3] Chute was a peculiar of the prebendary of Chute and Chisenbury. Jolly's subscription is not recorded in the dean's book.
[4] The presentation by the Crown was corroborative.

24 May 1635
583 Nathaniel Saunders, B.A. (Hart Hall, Oxf.), curate of Hungerford, Berks., ordained deacon.
    23 December 1638: vicar of Little Bedwyn, ordained priest. [*AO, WR*]
584 Edward Curtis, B.A. (Magdalen, Oxf.), curate of Faringdon, Berks., ordained deacon. [*AO*]
585 John Denison, M.A. (Balliol, Oxf.), ordained deacon.
    20 September 1635: curate of St. Lawrence's, Reading, Berks., ordained priest. [*AO*]
586 George Poulter, B.A. (Brasenose, Oxf.), curate of Winterslow, ordained deacon. [*AO*]
587 Edward Amye, M.A. (Christ's, Camb.), ordained priest. [*AC*]
588 Henry Pinnell, B.A. (St. Mary Hall, Oxf.), ordained deacon.
    23 September 1638: curate of Brinkworth, ordained priest. [*AO*]
[*and see* nos. 478, 552, 569]

25 May 1635
[*see* no. 538]

29 May 1635
589 Gilbert Wimberley, S.T.P., rector of Englefield, Berks. *Inst.* (f. 36) on the resignation of Robert Cottesford; patron, Ferdinando, Lord Hastings. *Comp.* (334/18 f. 152) 30 May 1635; sureties, Richard Gaunt, William Pitches. [*AO, WR* pp. 62–3]

29–31 May 1635[1]
590 William Williams, B.A., licensed to preach in the diocese. [? *ACO*]
[*and see* no. 310]

31 May 1635
591 Thomas Clerk, B.A., vicar of St. Mary's, Marlborough, licensed to preach in the diocese. [? *ACO*]

20 June 1635
592 John Penry, B.A., licensed to preach in the diocese.

2 June 1635[2]
593 Richard Cleark, M.A., licensed to preach in the diocese. [*AO*]

7 July 1635
594 Thomas Elson, [B.A.,] licensed to preach in the diocese.
    16 July 1640: rector of Oaksey (Wokesey). *Inst.* (f. 49) on the resignation of Thomas Yule; patrons, Killaway Gridott, William Gridott. [*AO*]

8 July 1635
595 William Charnbury, licensed to preach in the diocese.
    18 October 1639: rector of Stanton St. Quintin. *Inst.* (f. 47) on the death

---

[1] The position in the book of these subscriptions, which are undated, is a rough indication of their dates.
[2] It is not certain why this subscription is apparently out of chronological sequence. In Cleark's subscription 2 June is possibly a mistake for 22 June.

of Robert Merrick; patron, James Charnbury. *Comp.* (334/20 f. 51) 28 Apr. 1640; sureties, Bampfield Sidenham, John Ager. [*WR*]

9 July 1635
596 Redeemed (Redemptus) Compton, M.A., curate of Bray, Berks., licensed to preach in the diocese.

11 August 1635
[*see* no. 545]

11 September 1635
597 Peter Nicholls, M.A., rector of Little Hinton. *Inst.* (f. 36) on the death of Melchisedech Francis; patron, Walter, bishop of Winchester. *Comp.* (334/18 f. 158) 21 Sept. 1635; sureties, Thomas Rigbie, Richard Edlin. [*AO, PR*]

20 September 1635
598 William Bowman, M.A. (St. Mary Hall, Oxf.), ordained deacon.
   27 March 1637: licensed to preach in the diocese.
   22 September 1639: ordained priest. [*AO*]
599 William Pound, M.A. (St. Alban Hall, Oxf.), ordained priest. [*AO* (Pownde)]
600 Christopher Dugdale, B.A. (Balliol, Oxf.), ordained deacon.
   1 March 1640: curate of East Woodhay, Hants, ordained priest. [*AO* (Dugdayle)]
601 Thomas Twiss, B.A. (Magdalen, Oxf.), curate of Grittleton, ordained deacon.
   23 September 1638: ordained priest. [*AO*]
602 Jonas Lawrence, B.A. (Magdalen, Oxf.), curate of Great Somerford, ordained deacon.
603 Robert Kitson, B.A. (Oxf.), curate of Wargrave, Berks., ordained deacon. [*AO*]
604 William Collins, B.A. (Christ Church, Oxf.), curate of Cookham, Berks., ordained deacon. [*AO*]
[*and see* nos. 551, 564, 585]

30 September 1635
605 William Owen, M.A. (Queen's, Oxf.), licensed to preach in the diocese. [*AO*]

8 October 1635
[*see* no. 172]

18 November 1635
[*see* no. 581]

25 November 1635
[*see* no. 563]

8 December 1635
606 Edward Tutt, M.A., vicar of North Newnton. *Inst.* (f. 36) on the death

of John Cooper; patron, Philip, earl of Pembroke.
  20 December 1635: ordained priest. [*AO*, *PR*]
[*and see* no. 119]

20 December 1635
607 John Sweete, B.A., curate of Pertwood, ordained priest. [*AO*]
608 Richard Page, M.A., curate of Patney, ordained priest.
  20 June 1638: licensed to preach at Patney and in the diocese.
  3 December 1638: vicar of Whiteparish. *Inst.* (f. 45) on the death of
Silvester Goter; patron, John Poucherdon. *Comp.* (334/20 f. 21) 30 May
1639; sureties, Alexander Thayne, John Butler. [*AO*, *WR*]
609 John Pitt, M.A. (Hart Hall, Oxf.), ordained deacon. [*ACO*, *WR* p. 136]
610 Richard Hayter, M.A. (Magdalen, Oxf.), ordained deacon. [*AO*, *Conc.
Test.*, *DNB*]
611 Benjamin Maber, B.A. (New Inn Hall, Oxf.), ordained deacon.
  5 March 1637: curate of Stinsford, Dors., ordained priest. [*AO*]
612 William Hunt, M.A. (Trinity, Oxf.), curate of Buttermere, ordained
deacon.
  18 December 1636: ordained priest. [*AO*]
613 Richard Oxley, B.A. (Oxf.), curate of Cholsey, Berks., ordained deacon.
[*AO*]
614 Brian Alder, B.A. (Balliol, Oxf.), curate of Chaddleworth, Berks.,
ordained priest.
  11 May 1638: curate of Frilsham, Berks., licensed to preach in the diocese.
[*AO*]
615 Samuel Paine, B.A. (Brasenose, Oxf.), curate of Monkton Deverill,
ordained deacon.
  24 September 1637: ordained priest.
  25 September 1637: licensed to preach at Hamstead Marshall, Berks.,
and in the diocese. [*AO*, *WR* p. 317]
[*and see* no. 606]

7 January 1636
616 Henry Collier (Collyer), M.A., rector of Steeple Langford, licensed to
preach in the diocese. *Inst.* (f. 37) on the death of Joseph Collyer; patron,
Henry Miles. *Comp.* (334/18 f. 169) 4 Feb. 1636; sureties, Joseph Collyer,
George Clove. [*AO*, *PR*, *WR*]
[*and see* no. 491]

9 February 1636
[*see* no. 420]

10 March 1636
617 John Bernarde (Barnard), M.A., vicar of Berwick St. James. *Inst.* (f. 37)
on the death of Richard Mayle; patron, Henry Sandys. [*AO*, *PR*]

13 March 1636
618 Thomas Dove, M.A. (Magdalen, Oxf.), ordained deacon.
  24 September 1637: ordained priest. [*AO*]

619 Richard Levett, M.A. (Magdalen, Oxf.), curate of Collingbourne Ducis, ordained priest. [*AO, CR* p. 324]

620 Robert Burdon, M.A. (Magdalen, Oxf.), curate of Stanton St. Bernard, ordained deacon. [*AO*]

621 Thomas Payne, M.A. (Magdalen, Oxf.), ordained deacon. [*AO, WR* p. 70]

622 Thomas Bisse, B.A. (Oriel, Oxf.), curate of Bishopstrow, ordained deacon. [*AO*][1]

623 Thomas Horne, [B.A.] (St. Edmund Hall, Oxf.), curate of Somerford, ordained deacon. [*AO*]

624 John Barrett, M.A. (St. Edmund Hall, Oxf.), curate of Mere, ordained priest. [*AO*]

625 Adam Ranger, M.A. (Balliol, Oxf.), curate of Fugglestone, ordained priest. [*AO*]
[*and see* no. 443]

13 April 1636
[*see* no. 101]

14 May 1636
626 Benjamin Some, [M.A.,] vicar of Shalbourne, Berks. No subscription or institution.[2] *Comp.* (334/18 f. 175); sureties, Maximilian Bard, Edward Denman. [*AC*]

18 May 1636
[*see* no. 86]

3 June 1636
627 William Gunn (Gunne), M.A., vicar of Marden. *Inst.* (f. 38) on the death of William Davyd; patrons, the dean and chapter of Bristol. [*AO, PR*]

7 June 1636
628 Edmund Kynnesman, M.A., vicar of Steventon, Berks. *Inst.* (f. 38); patron, the bishop, through lapse.[3] [*AC* (Kinsman)]

12 June 1636
629 Edward Hyde, M.A. (Christ Church, Oxf.), ordained deacon.
   18 December 1636: ordained priest.
   2 September 1637: rector of West Grimstead. *Inst.* (f. 41) on the resignation of William Barlowe; patron, Laurence Hyde. *Comp.* (334/18 f. 213) 31 Oct. 1637; sureties, John Semtloe, James Goldston. [*AO, WR*]

630 Walter Bushnell, M.A. (Magdalen, Oxf.), curate of Box, ordained deacon. [*AO* (Bushell), *DNB, WR*]

---

1 Bisse's living was sequestrated in 1646 but restored 1660: *V.C.H. Wilts.* viii. 11.
2 Shalbourne was a peculiar of the dean and canons of Windsor. Some subscribed before the dean of Salisbury 28 Apr. 1636.
3 The patron was John Williams, bishop of Lincoln (see nos. 309, 371, 482), who in July 1636 was facing charges which led to his imprisonment in 1637: *D.N.B.*

631 Thomas Hitchcock (Hitchcocke), B.A. (Exeter, Oxf.), curate of Alton Barnes, ordained deacon.

22 December 1639: curate of Alton Priors [Overton parish],[1] ordained priest. [*AO*]

632 Samuel Rogers, M.A., Fellow of Queens', Camb., ordained priest. [*AO, FS, WR*]

633 Richard Rocke, M.A., Scholar of Wadham, Oxf., ordained deacon. [*AO, WR* p. 136]

634 William Langley, M.A. (Pembroke, Oxf.), curate of Brightwell, Berks., ordained priest. [*AO, WR* p. 324]

635 Thomas Banning, B.A. (Magdalen, Oxf.), curate of Winterbourne Monkton, ordained deacon.

23 September 1638: ordained priest. [*AO*]
[*and see* nos. 544, 570]

8 July 1636

636 Henry Carpenter, M.A., vicar of Steeple Ashton. *Inst.* (f. 38) on the promotion of George Webb as bishop of Limerick; patron, the Crown. *Comp.* (334/18 f. 182) 19 July 1636; sureties, Francis Rowland, Thomas Massie.

12 December 1638: rector of Hilperton. *Inst.* (f. 45) on the death of Henry Hulbert; patron, Edward Long. *Comp.* (334/20 f. 1) 14 Jan. 1639; sureties, Samuel Martyn, Thomas Massie. [*AO, FS, PR*]

9 July 1636

637 Samuel Marsh, S.T.B., prebendary of Ruscombe. *Inst.* (f. 38) on the resignation of Samuel Marsh; patron, the bishop.

27 June 1639: rector of Patney. *Inst.* (f. 47) on the promotion of James Wedderburne as bishop of Dunblane; patron, the Crown. *Comp.* (334/20 f. 34) 4 Nov. 1639; sureties, James Marsh, Robert Marsh. [*AO, FS, PR, WR*]

26 July 1636
[*see* no. 340]

18 August 1636
[*see* no. 474]

25 September 1636[2]

638 William Eyre, M.A. (Magdalen, Oxf.), ordained deacon. [*AO, PR, CR* p. 187]

639 Samuel Welles, M.A. (Magdalen, Oxf.), curate of Ashbury, Berks., ordained deacon. [*AO, CR* p. 520]

640 Grindall Sheaf (Sheafe), M.A., Fellow of King's, Camb., ordained deacon.

18 February 1638: ordained priest. [*AC, PR, WR* p. 272]

641 William Swayne, M.A., vicar of Cranborne, Dors., ordained priest. [*AO*]

---

[1] The churches of Alton Barnes and Alton Priors are less than ¼ mile apart.
[2] The reasons for the unusually many subscriptions for Dorset 25 Sept. are given on p. 4.

642 William Barlow, M.A. (New Inn Hall, Oxf.), ordained deacon.

28 April 1637: licensed to preach at St. Mary's, Wallingford, Berks., and in the archdeaconry of Berkshire.

23 September 1638: curate of Melksham, ordained priest. [*AO*]

643 John Jesope, B.A. (Christ Church, Oxf.), curate of West Parley, Dors., ordained priest. [*AO* (Jessop), *WR* p. 372]

644 Edward Ancketyll, B.A. (St. Edmund Hall, Oxf.), curate of Wareham, Dors., ordained deacon.

645 William South, B.A. (St. Edmund Hall, Oxf.), ordained deacon. [*AO*]

646 Robert Head, B.A. (New Inn Hall, Oxf.), curate of Berwick St. James, ordained deacon. [*AO*]

647 John Sacheverell, B.A. (New Inn Hall, Oxf.), curate of Bere Regis, Dors., ordained deacon.

24 September 1637: ordained priest. [*AO*, *CR* p. 422, *DNB* (s.v. Henry Sacheverell)]

648 John Larder, M.A. (Wadham, Oxf.), ordained priest. [*AO*]

649 Robert Parker, B.A. (Wadham, Oxf.), curate of Cranborne, Dors., ordained deacon. [*AO*]

650 Edward Heighmore, B.A. (Gloucester Hall, Oxf.), curate of Stickland, Dors., ordained deacon.

651 Francis Ward, B.A. (Hart Hall, Oxf.), curate of Manston, Dors., ordained deacon. [*AO*, *WR* p. 138]

652 Francis Moore, B.A. (Gloucester Hall, Oxf.), curate of Sedgehill,[1] ordained deacon. [*AO*]

[*and see* no. 540]

29 October 1636

653 Jerameel Terrent, M.A., vicar of Winkfield, Berks. *Inst.* (f. 39) 19 Oct. 1636 on a death; patrons, the dean and chapter of Salisbury. [*AO* (Tarrant), *FS*]

3 November 1636

654 John Stanley, M.A., vicar of Hullavington. *Inst.* (f. 39) on the death of John Moore; patron, Eton College. [*AO*, *PR*, *WR* p. 399]

9 December 1636

[*see* no. 208]

18 December 1636

655 Giles Thornburgh, B.A. (New Inn Hall, Oxf.), ordained priest.

6 July 1636: rector of Orcheston St. Mary. *Inst.* (f. 40) on the death of Giles Thornburgh;[2] patron, Laurence Clifton. *Comp.* (334/18 f. 214) 7 Nov. 1637; sureties, Laurence Clifton, Henry Oldham. [*AO*, *FS*, *WR*]

656 Thomas Boult, B.A. (Hart Hall, Oxf.), curate of Shrewton, ordained deacon. [*AO*]

---

[1] See no. 76 n.

[2] Father of the subscriber: *AO*, *WR*.

657 Peter Blanchard, M.A. (Trinity, Oxf.), curate of Ludgershall, ordained deacon.

24 December 1637: ordained priest. [*AO*]

658 Christopher Mervin, M.A. (Magdalen, Oxf.), curate of Bishopstone, ordained deacon.

24 December 1637: ordained priest. [*AO*]

659 Edward Hinton, M.A., Fellow of Merton, Oxf., ordained deacon.

22 September 1639: ordained priest. [*AO*]

660 John Bygge, B.A. (Brasenose, Oxf.), curate of Idstone (Higston) [Ashbury parish],[1] Berks., ordained deacon.

10 March 1639: curate of Winterslow, ordained priest. [*AO*]

[*and see* nos. 612, 629]

25 January 1637

661 Richard Bridges, B.A., rector of Ditteridge. *Inst.* (f. 39); patron, George Speke.

11 October 1639: rector of Monkton Farleigh. *Inst.* (f. 47) on the death of Lewis Jones; patron, the Crown. *Comp.* (334/20 f. 34) 9 Nov. 1639; sureties, George Clove, William Foster. [*AO, PR*]

4 February 1637

[*see* no. 252]

13 February 1637

[*see* no. 8]

25 February 1637

662 John Fabian, M.A., rector of Nettleton. *Inst.* (f. 40) on the death of Laurence Barlow; patron, Sir John St. John. *Comp.* (334/18 f. 202) 16 May 1637; sureties, Henry Fabian, Edward Fabian. *Inst.* (f. 41) 29 Sept. 1637; patron, the Crown.[2] [*AO, PR*]

5 March 1637

663 Henry Cusse, M.A. (Hart Hall, Oxf.), ordained priest.

20 June 1638: licensed to preach at North Tidworth and in the diocese. [*AO, Conc. Test., CR* p. 155]

664 Ambrose Clare, B.A. (New Inn Hall, Oxf.), ordained deacon. [*ACO, CR* p. 116]

665 Christopher Fowler, M.A. (St. Edmund Hall, Oxf.), ordained deacon.

24 December 1637: curate of Welford, Berks., ordained priest.

10 June 1640: rector of West Woodhay, Berks. *Inst.* (f. 49) on the death of John Squire; patron, John Fowler. [*AO, CR* pp. 208–9, *DNB*]

666 John Sharpe, B.A. (Magdalen, Oxf.), curate of Porton [Idmiston parish], ordained deacon. [*AO, Conc. Test.*]

667 John Michael (Michaell), B.A. (Balliol, Oxf.), ordained deacon. [*AO*]

[*and see* nos. 474, 611]

---

1 There was a medieval oratory at Idstone: *V.C.H. Berks.* ii. 12 n.
2 The presentation by the Crown was corroborative.

16 March 1637
668 William Noble, M.A., vicar of Sutton Benger. *Inst.* (f. 40) on the death of Simon Yorke; patron, the bishop. [*AO, PR*]

27 March 1637
[*see* no. 598]

28 April 1637
[*see* no. 642]

18 May 1637
[*see* no. 468]

19 May 1637
[*see* nos. 147, 468][1]

26 May 1637
669 William White, M.A., rector of Wargrave, Berks. *Inst.* (f. 40); patron, the Crown. *Comp.* (334/18 f. 215) 11 Nov. 1637; sureties, John Chase, William Kirby. [*AO*]

4 June 1637
670 Robert Filkes, M.A. (Magdalen, Oxf.), curate of Yatton Keynell, ordained deacon.
    9 June 1639: ordained priest. [*AO*]
671 Henry Lambe, B.A. (New Inn Hall, Oxf.), curate of St. Peter's, Marlborough, ordained deacon. [*AO*]
672 Richard Coxe, B.A. (St. Edmund Hall, Oxf.), curate of Norton Coleparle, ordained deacon.
    18 February 1638: ordained priest. [*AO*]
673 Maurice (Morris) Roberts, B.A. (Jesus, Oxf.), curate of East Garston, Berks., ordained deacon.
    20 May 1638: ordained priest.
    20 May 1638: licensed to preach in the diocese.[2]
674 Thomas Bright, M.A. (Trinity, Oxf.), curate of Shottesbrook, Berks., ordained deacon.
    18 February 1638: curate of Waltham Abbots, Berks., ordained priest. [*AO*]
675 John Lyddall, M.A. (St. Edmund Hall, Oxf.), curate of Chirton, ordained deacon. [*AO*]
[*and see* no. 498]

23 June 1637
676 Richard Anyan, S.T.B., rector of South Moreton, Berks. *Inst.* (f. 40) on the death of Charles Sagler; patron, John Holloway.
    8 May 1638: licensed to preach in the diocese. [*AO*]

---

1 The subscriptions of the new sub-dean and prebendary of Bedminster and Ratcliffe after the death of Giles Thornburgh.
2 Separate subscriptions were made for the ordination and licensing.

13 July 1637
677 Samuel Kinaston, M.A., rector of Great Somerford. *Inst.* (f. 41) 16 July 1637 on the death of John Langton; patron, the Crown. *Comp.* (334/18 f. 210) 16 Aug. 1637; sureties, Thomas Kynaston, Edward Powell. [*AO, PR*]

17 July 1637
678 Robert Bower, M.A., rector of Great Wishford. *Inst.* (f. 41) on the death of John Bower; patron, William Bower. *Comp.* (334/18 f. 208) 25 July 1637; sureties, John Greenhill, Abraham Porter.
   24 September 1637: ordained priest.
   26 April 1638: licensed to preach in the diocese. [*AO, FS, PR, WR*]

2 August 1637
679 Thomas Saxby, [M.A.,] vicar of Sonning, Berks. No subscription or institution.[1] *Comp.* (334/18 f. 209); sureties, John Bunburie, Nathaniel Smith. [*AO*]

10 August 1637
680 Christopher Young (Yonge), M.A., rector of Odstock. *Inst.* (f. 41) on the death of Giles Thornburgh; patron, Wilfred Young. *Comp.* (334/18 f. 213) 31 Oct. 1637; sureties, John Haviland, Hugh Perry. [*AO, PR*]

18 August 1637
[*see* no. 555]

28 August 1637
[*see* no. 235]

2 September 1637
[*see* no. 629]

23 September 1637
681 John Gandy (Gandye), M.A., prebendary of Torleton. *Inst.* (f. 41) on a death;[2] patron, the bishop. [*AO*]

24 September 1637
682 John Bishop, B.A. (Hart Hall, Oxf.), curate of Stanton by Highworth, ordained priest. [*AO*]
683 Nathaniel Nicholas, B.A. (Emmanuel, Camb.), curate of Sutton, Winchester diocese, ordained deacon.
   24 December 1637: ordained priest. [*CR* p. 365]
684 Neville Heath, B.A. (Clare, Camb.), ordained deacon. [*AC*]
685 Richard Gillingham, B.A. (Gonville and Caius, Camb.), curate of Woodford, ordained deacon. [*AC, WR* p. 132]
686 Thomas Hill, M.A. (Magdalen, Oxf.), ordained deacon.
   23 December 1638: curate of Baverstock, ordained priest. [*AO, FS, PR, ? WR* p. 374]
[*and see* nos. 615, 618, 647, 678]

---

[1] Sonning was a peculiar of the dean, before whom Saxby subscribed 20 July 1637.
[2] Probably that of William Hicks: no. 167.

25 September 1637
[*see* no. 615]

7 October 1637
[*see* no. 462]

14 October 1637
[*see* no. 362]

14 November 1637
[*see* no. 504]

8 December 1637
687 John Chalkhill, M.A., vicar of Downton. *Inst.* (f. 42) on the death of William Wilks; patron, Winchester College. *Comp.* (334/18 f. 230) 18 Apr. 1638; sureties, Edward Betts, John Dennet. [*AO, PR*]

10 December 1637
[*see* no. 578]

24 December 1637
688 William Gilpin, B.A. (St. Edmund Hall, Oxf.), curate of Norton, ordained deacon.
689 John Guy, B.A. (Hart Hall, Oxf.), curate of Wadeford [Chard parish], Som., ordained deacon. [*AO*]
690 John Swayne, B.C.L. (Pembroke, Oxf.), curate of Urchfont, ordained deacon. [*AO*]
691 Thomas Blagrave, M.A. (St. Mary Hall, Oxf.), curate of Chieveley, Berks., ordained deacon.
   20 May 1638: ordained priest. [*AO*]
692 Richard Price, M.A. (Balliol, Oxf.), curate of Farnborough, Berks., ordained deacon. [*AO*]
693 Walter Paine, B.A. (Trinity, Oxf.), curate of Monkton Deverill, ordained deacon. [*AO*]
694 William Thornburgh, M.A. (New Inn Hall, Oxf.), curate of Orcheston St. George, ordained deacon. [*AO*, ? *WR* p. 246]
695 John Barlowe, M.A. (Brasenose, Oxf.), curate of Boxford, Berks., ordained deacon.
   18 February 1638: licensed to baptize infants and to preach at Boxford.[1]
   23 December 1638: ordained priest. [*AO*, ? *WR* p. 16]
696 Robert Olden, B.A. (Hart Hall, Oxf.), curate of Chilmark, ordained deacon. [*AO, WR* (Oldinge) p. 378]
[*and see* nos. 345, 362, 399, 657–8, 665, 683]

29 December 1637
697 Edward Lyford, M.A., rector of Peasemore, Berks. *Inst.* (f. 42) on the resignation of William Lyford; patron, Richard Lyford. *Comp.* (334/18 f. 224) 17 Feb. 1638; sureties, Bernard Lyford, Edward Weld. [*AO*]

---

1 This is the only example in the bishops' book of such a licence being granted. Deacons were allowed to minister the sacrament of baptism only in the absence of the priest.

4 January 1638
698 Thomas Hochkis (Hotchkiss), M.A., rector of Stanton by Highworth. *Inst.* (f. 42) on the death of John Woodbridge; patron, John Ayrgun. *Comp.* (334/18 f. 222) 12 Jan. 1638; sureties, John Taylor, senior, John Taylor, junior.
    18 May 1638: licensed to preach in the diocese. [*AC, Conc. Test., PR*]

12 January 1638
699 Herbert Croft, S.T.B. (Christ Church, Oxf.), ordained priest.
    1 August 1639: prebendary of Minor Pars Altaris. *Inst.* (f. 47) on the resignation of William Tounson; patron, the bishop. [*AO, DNB, FS, WR* p. 8]

18 February 1638
700 Francis Williams, B.A. (Hart Hall, Oxf.), ordained deacon.
701 Daniel Smith, B.A. (Magdalen, Oxf.), curate of Bremhill, ordained deacon. [*AO, WR* p. 8]
702 John Randall, B.A. (Lincoln, Oxf.), curate of Ogbourne, in the dean's jurisdiction, ordained priest.[1] [*AO,* ? *WR* p. 318]
703 John Clarke, B.A. (Magdalen, Oxf.), ordained deacon. [*AO,* ? *CR*]
[*and see* nos. 497, 602, 640, 672, 674, 695]

24 February 1638
[*see* no. 362]

12 March 1638
[*see* no. 557]

20 March 1638
704 John Littleton, S.T.P., vicar of Tilehurst, Berks. *Inst.* (f. 43) on the death of John, bishop of Rochester; patron, the Crown. *Comp.* (334/18 f. 231) 30 Apr. 1638; sureties, Timothy Littleton, James Lloyd. [*AO, WR* p. 53]

28 March 1638
[*see* nos. 122, 299]

26 April 1638
[*see* no. 678]

8 May 1638
705 Nicholas Young (Yonge), M.A., curate of Remenham, Berks., licensed to preach in the diocese. [*AO*]
[*and see* no. 676]

9 May 1638
706 John Wylmer, M.A., licensed to preach in the diocese. [*AO* (Wilmer), *CR*]

---

[1] Ogbourne St. Andrew and Ogbourne St. George were both under the jurisdiction of the dean and canons of Windsor. All candidates for ordination should have subscribed before the bishop.

10 May 1638
707 Giles Bingley, M.A., licensed to preach in the diocese. [*AO*]

11 May 1638
708 John Brackin, M.A., curate of East Ilsley, Berks., licensed to preach in the diocese. [*AC*]
[*and see* no. 614]

14 May 1638
709 John Crakanthorpe (Crackenthorpe), M.A., rector of Ashley. *Inst.* (f. 43) on the death of Robert Price; patron, the Crown. *Comp.* (334/18 f. 236) 15 June 1638; sureties, Thomas Kenn, Thomas Crakenthorpe. [*AC, PR*]

16 May 1638
710 Thomas Hancock, B.A. (Exeter, Oxf.), curate of Langley Burrell, licensed to preach in the diocese.
22 September 1639: ordained priest. [*AO, PR*]
711 Peter Glasbrooke, B.A., licensed to preach in the diocese. [*AO*]
712 Henry Storke, M.A., curate of Grittleton, licensed to preach in the diocese. [*AO, WR* pp. 319–20]

17 May 1638
[*see* no. 569]

18 May 1638
713 John Frayne, B.A., curate of Inglesham, licensed to preach in the diocese.
[*and see* no. 698]

20 May 1638
714 William Durham, M.A., curate of St. Mary's, Reading, Berks., ordained priest. [*AO, CR* pp. 174–5, *DNB*]
715 Joseph Barnes, M.A. (Magdalen, Oxf.), curate of East Ilsley, Berks., ordained deacon.
22 March 1639: rector of East Ilsley, Berks.
9 June 1639: ordained priest. [*ACO, WR*]
716 John Jaques, B.A. (Brasenose, Oxf.), curate of Aston Upthorpe [Blewbury parish], Berks., ordained deacon. [? *CR* p. 295]
717 John Reade, M.A. (Balliol, Oxf.), curate of Little Wittenham, Berks., ordained priest. [*AO*]
718 Thomas Bird (Byrd), M.A. (Magdalen, Oxf.), curate of Wasing, Berks., ordained deacon.
29 May 1638: vicar of Brimpton, Berks. *Inst.* (f. 43) on the resignation of John Squier; patrons, Sir Thomas Dachell, Richard Lybbe, and Thomas Howard.
10 March 1639: ordained priest. [*AO*]
719 Josiah White, M.A. (Magdalen, Oxf.), ordained deacon. [*AO*]
720 Edward Perkins, M.A. (Magdalen, Oxf.), curate of Sutton Courtenay, Berks., ordained priest. [*AO, CR* pp. 386–7]

721 Edward Hyde, M.A., Fellow of Trinity, Camb., ordained deacon.
23 September 1638: ordained priest. [*AC, DNB,* ? *WR* p. 69]
722 John Harmar, M.A. (St. Alban Hall, Oxf.), ordained deacon. [*AO*]
723 Humphrey Smith, M.A. (Exeter, Oxf.), curate of Little Somerford, ordained deacon. [*AO*]
724 Robert Albright, M.A. (Gloucester Hall, Oxf.), curate of Whiteparish, ordained deacon.
9 June 1639: curate of Patney, ordained priest. [*AO, WR* p. 369]
725 Thomas Helliar, B.A. (Trinity, Oxf.), curate of Sopworth, ordained deacon. [*AO*]
726 Thomas Collyer, B.A. (Hart Hall, Oxf.), curate of Bremhill, ordained deacon.
10 March 1639: ordained priest. [*AO*]
727 Leonard Clotworthy, B.A. (New Inn Hall, Oxf.), curate of Lytchett Minster, Dors., ordained priest.[1] [*AO*]
728 Nicholas Watts (Trinity, Oxf.),[2] curate of Donhead St. Andrew, ordained priest. [*AO*]
729 Thomas Watts, M.A. (Hart Hall, Oxf.), curate of Chippenham, ordained deacon. [*AO*]
730 Nicholas Sheppard (Shepherd), B.A. (King's, Camb.), ordained priest.
18 October 1638: vicar of Sutton Courtenay, Berks. *Inst.* (f. 44) on the death of Thomas Charles; patrons, the dean and chapter of Windsor.
22 October 1638: licensed to preach in the diocese. [*AC, WR*]
731 Henry Bennett (St. Mary Hall, Oxf.),[3] curate of Fugglestone, ordained deacon. [*AO*]
732 John Fulford, M.A. (Magdalene, Camb.), curate of Dunsford, Devon, ordained deacon. [*AC*]
733 Peter Gaisdon, M.A., licensed to preach at Donhead St. Mary and in the diocese. [*AO*]
[*and see* nos. 673, 691]

29 May 1638
[*see* no. 718]

20 June 1638
[*see* nos. 608, 663]

25 June 1638
[*see* no. 35]

3 July 1638
734 John Dearinge, B.A., curate of East Hagbourne, Berks., licensed to preach in the diocese.

---

1 Cf. no. 364. It is possible that nos. 364 and 727 are subscriptions by the same man but the interval of 8 years between deaconing and priesting diminishes the possibility.
2 Watts matriculated but apparently did not graduate: *AO*.
3 Bennett matriculated but apparently did not graduate: *AO*.

18 July 1638

735 Thomas Taylor, M.A., licensed to preach in the diocese. [*AO, CR* pp. 478–9]

20 July 1638

736 William Chillingworth, M.A., chancellor of Salisbury cathedral, prebendary of Brixworth. *Inst.* (f. 43) on the promotion of Brian Duppa as bishop of Chichester. *Comp.* (334/20 f. 2) 30 Jan. 1639; sureties, John Littleton, Francis Chillingworth. [*ACO, DNB, FS, WR* p. 233]

23 September 1638

737 Edward Lin (Line, Lynne), B.A. (Clare, Camb.), ordained deacon. [*AC, CR* p. 325]

738 Francis Beyley, B.A., Fellow of New, Oxf., ordained deacon.

6 October 1638: vicar of Berwick St. James. *Inst.* (f. 43) on the cession of John Bernard; patron, Henry Sandys. [*AO, FS, PR*]

739 Richard Saxe, M.A. (Brasenose, Oxf.), curate of Chilton Foliat, ordained deacon.

740 Thomas Horne, M.A. (Queen's, Oxf.), curate of Stratfield Mortimer, Berks., ordained deacon. [*AO, WR* p. 185]

741 Thomas Otway, B.A. (Christ's, Camb.), curate of Rockbourne, Hants, ordained deacon. [*AC, WR* p. 402]

742 William Elks, M.A. (Balliol, Oxf.), curate of Enborne, Berks., ordained deacon. [*AO*]

743 John Mosely (Moseley), B.A. (New Inn Hall, Oxf.), curate of Woodford, ordained deacon. [*AO*]

744 Thomas Tyrer, B.A. (New Inn Hall, Oxf.), curate of Midgham [Thatcham parish], Berks., ordained deacon.

1 March 1640: curate of Little Coxwell, Berks., ordained priest. [*AO*]

745 Ralph Tounson, B.A. (Pembroke, Camb.), curate of Upway, Dors., ordained deacon.

22 September 1639: ordained priest. [*AC, WR*]

746 John Greene, M.A. (Magdalen, Oxf.), ordained deacon. [*AO*]

747 John Walton, B.A. (Trinity, Camb.), curate of Whitchurch, Dors., ordained deacon. [*AC*]

[*and see* nos. 574, 601, 635, 642, 721]

6 October 1638

[*see* no. 738]

9 October 1638

748 John Brooker, M.A., rector of Sulham, Berks. *Inst.* (f. 44) on the death of William Wolfe; patrons, John Brooker and William Pococke. [*AO*]

10 October 1638

749 John Hieron (Hern, Hearn), M.A., vicar of Sherston Magna. *Inst.* (f. 44) on the deprivation of Samuel Dowling; patron, William Kemp. *Comp.* (334/18 f. 249) 20 Nov. 1638; sureties, Richard Thorner, Nathan Smith.

28 October 1640: rector of Garsdon. No subscription.[1] *Inst.* (f. 50) on the death of Richard Woodroffe; patron, William Palmer. *Comp.* (334/20 f. 76) 15 Feb. 1641; sureties, John Meremonth, Richard Franklin. [*AO, PR, WR*]

11 October 1638
[*see* no. 132]

18 October 1638
[*see* nos. 425, 730]

22 October 1638
[*see* no. 730]

24 October 1638
750 Richard Wright, B.A., rector of Tidmarsh, Berks. *Inst.* (f. 44) on the death of William Wolf; patrons, Anthony White and Robert Martin. [*AO*]

30 November 1638
[*see* no. 197]

3 December 1638
[*see* no 608]

11 December 1638
751 Simon Croker, B A., vicar of Corsham. *Inst.* (f. 45) on the death of Humphrey Paget; patron, Sir Edward Hungerford. *Comp.* (334/20 f. 8) 28 Feb. 1639; sureties, John Hungerford, Giles Hungerford. [*AO, Conc. Test., PR, WR* p. 372]

12 December 1638
[*see* no. 636]

23 December 1638
752 Thomas Blanchard, M.A. (Pembroke, Oxf.), curate of North Wraxall, ordained deacon.
    23 December 1639: rector of North Wraxall, ordained priest. *Inst.* (f. 48) on the death of Thomas Blanchard; patron, Thomas Clayton. *Comp.* (334/20 f. 41) 14 Jan. 1640; sureties, Richard Blanchard, James Prince. [*AO*]
753 Thomas Webbe, M.A. (Balliol, Oxf.), curate of Castle Combe, ordained deacon. [*AO*]
754 Edward Onslow, M.A. (St. Mary Hall, Oxf.), ordained priest. [*AO, FS, WR* p. 175]
755 William Parry, M.A. (Hart Hall, Oxf.), curate of Martin [Damerham parish],[2] ordained priest. [*AO, WR* p. 379]
756 Henry Clifford, M.A. (Sidney Sussex, Camb.), curate of Ibsley, Hants, ordained priest. [*AC*]
757 William Grove, M.A. (Wadham, Oxf.), ordained deacon.
    9 June 1639: ordained priest. [*AO, FS, WR* p. 373]

1 The last recorded subscription before Davenant is dated 5 Aug. 1640.
2 See no. 390 n.

758 Richard Hippsley, M.A. (Trinity, Oxf.), curate of Brightwell, Berks., ordained deacon. [AO]

759 Andrew Dominicke, M.A. (Pembroke, Oxf.), curate of South Hinksey, Berks., ordained deacon. [AO]

760 Marmaduke Goode, B.A. (Queen's, Oxf.), curate of Englefield, Berks., ordained deacon.

22 December 1639: ordained priest. [AO, FS]

761 Henry Green (Greene), Scholar of Magdalen, Oxf., curate of Shaw, Berks., ordained deacon. [AO]

[and see nos. 397, 554, 583, 686, 695]

24 December 1638
[see no. 397]

27 December 1638
[see no. 321]

5 January 1639
[see nos. 125, 147]

8 January 1639
762 John Bott, B.A., rector of Remenham, Berks. *Inst.* (f. 45) on the death of John King; patron, John Lovelace. *Comp.* (334/20 f. 5) 12 Feb. 1639; sureties, John Andrewes, Richard Waynmer. [AC]

15 January 1639
[see no. 197]

30 January 1639
763 Richard Clayton, M.A., rector of Shellingford, Berks. *Inst.* (f. 46) on the death of John Parkhurst; patron, John Parker. *Comp.* (334/20 f. 7) 27 Feb. 1639; sureties, Richard Woolton, Daniel Holdenby. [AO, FS]

27 February 1639
764 Joseph Gulson (Gulston), S.T.B., rector of Fonthill Bishop. *Inst.* (f. 46) on a cession;[1] patron, Walter, bishop of Winchester. *Comp.* (334/20 f. 12) 10 Apr. 1639; sureties, William Mogg, Robert Bower. [AC, PR, WR p. 183]

7 March 1639
[see no. 460]

10 March 1639
765 Richard Goddard, M.A. (Pembroke, Oxf.), curate of Burghclere, Hants, ordained priest. [AO]

766 Richard Kent, M.A. (St. Alban Hall, Oxf.), curate of Rollestone, ordained deacon. [AO, FS, WR p. 375]

767 Benedict Barrow, B.A. (St. John's, Camb.), curate of Brean, Som., ordained deacon.

1 March 1640: curate of Bramshaw, ordained priest. [AC]

768 Nathaniel Tucker, B.A. (New Inn Hall, Oxf.), ordained deacon. [AO]

---

[1] Possibly that of Christopher Wren: no. 18.

769 Richard South, M.A. (Magdalen, Oxf.), ordained deacon. [*AO*]

770 John Horspoole, B.A. (Lincoln, Oxf.), curate of Newton Valence, Hants, ordained deacon.

1 March 1640: curate of Kingsley, Hants, ordained priest. [*AO*]
[*and see* nos. 660, 718, 726]

19 March 1639
771 Walter Clark, S.T.B., rector of Burghfield, Berks. *Inst.* (f. 46) on the death of Gilbert Johnson; patron, Martin Wright. *Comp.* (334/20 f. 10) 21 Mar. 1639; sureties, Nicholas Clarke, William Clark.

27 March 1639: rector of Burghfield, Berks. *Inst.* (f. 46) on the death of Gilbert Johnson; patron, Martin Wright.[1] [*ACO*]

22 March 1639
[*see* no. 715]

27 March 1639
[*see* no. 771]

24 May 1639
[*see* no. 514]

6 June 1639
772 John Earle, M.A., rector and vicar of Bishopstone.[2] *Inst.* (f. 47) on the death of William Helm; patron, Philip, earl of Pembroke. *Comp.* (334/20 f. 33) 30 Oct. 1639; sureties, John Graunte, John Leigh. [*AO, DNB, FS, PR, WR*]

9 June 1639
773 Peter Coxe, B.A. (Sidney Sussex, Camb.), curate of Broadwindsor, Dors., ordained deacon. [*AC, WR* p. 311]

774 John Hinckley, B.A. (St. Alban Hall, Oxf.), curate of Hatford, Berks., ordained deacon. [*AO, DNB*]

775 Jerome (Jeronymus) Turner, B.A. (Wadham, Oxf.), curate of Over Compton, Dors., ordained priest. [*AO*]

776 John Barnes, *litteratus* (New Inn Hall, Oxf.), curate of Maiden Bradley, ordained priest. [*AO*]

777 Griffin Ward, Scholar of Magdalen, Oxf., curate of Aldworth, Berks., ordained deacon.

778 Walter Pitman, B.A. (St. Edmund Hall, Oxf.), curate of Lydiard Millicent, ordained deacon. [*AO*]

779 John Watts, B.A. (Trinity, Oxf.), curate of Donhead St. Andrew, ordained deacon. [*AO*, ? *CR* p. 514]
[*and see* nos. 670, 715, 724, 757]

27 June 1639
[*see* no. 637]

---

1 The reasons for the double subscription and institution are not clear.
2 The rectory and vicarage of Bishopstone in Downton hundred were held separately in the Middle Ages but together from at least the early 17th century: *PR*, ii. 7.

1 August 1639
[see no. 699]

22 September 1639
780 Anthony Woodman, B.A. (Pembroke, Oxf.), curate of Bradford on Avon, ordained deacon. [AO]
781 Uriah Banks, M.A. (Brasenose, Oxf.), curate of Wilton, ordained deacon. [AO, PR]
782 John Payne, M.A. (New Inn Hall, Oxf.), curate of Cookham, Berks., ordained priest. [AO]
783 George Lisle, M.A. (Balliol, Oxf.), curate of Odstock, ordained deacon. [AO, CR p. 325]
784 Dositheus Palmer, M.A. (Magdalen, Oxf.), curate of Hilmarton, ordained deacon. [AO]
[and see nos. 598, 659, 710, 745]

11 October 1639
[see no. 661]

18 October 1639
[see no. 595]

8 November 1639
785 John Vincent, M.A., prebendary of Netheravon. *Inst.* (f. 47) on the resignation of Robert Pearson; patron, the bishop. [ACO, FS]

21 November 1639
786 Thomas Hyde, M.A., prebendary of Stratford sub Castle. *Inst.* (f. 48) on the resignation of Charles Robson; patron, the bishop. [AO FS, WR p. 185]

22 November 1639
787 Thomas Earle, [B.A.,] rector of Shorncote. *Inst.* (f. 48) on the death of John Snead; patron, Spencer, earl of Northampton. [AO (Earnley), PR, WR]

16 December 1639
788 Francis Mundy, M.A., rector of Welford, Berks., licensed to preach in the diocese. *Inst.* (f. 48) on the death of Thomas Sheafe; patron, Thomas Husey. *Comp.* (334/20 f. 44) 19 Feb. 1640; sureties, Thomas Husey, Tobias Katewell. [AO]

22 December 1639
789 Timothy Dewell, M.A. (Magdalen, Oxf.), curate of Rodbourne Cheney, ordained deacon. [AO]
790 Thomas Byrom, M.A. (Brasenose, Oxf.), curate of Bishop's Lavington, ordained deacon. [AO, WR]
791 John Duke, M.A. (Pembroke, Oxf.), ordained deacon. [AO]
792 John Hannam, M.A. (St. Alban Hall, Oxf.), curate of Teffont, ordained priest. [AO, WR p. 184]
793 Robert Haysome, LL.B., late of New, Oxf., now of Lincoln, Oxf., ordained deacon. [AO (Haysham), WR p. 184]

794 William Smallwood, B.A. (Balliol, Oxf.), curate of Marlston [Bucklebury parish], Berks., ordained deacon. [*AO*]

795 William Hughes, B.A. (New Inn Hall, Oxf.), curate of Bromham, ordained deacon. [*AO, CR* pp. 282–3]

796 Henry Welsteed, B.A. (Brasenose, Oxf.), curate of Froyle, [Hants,] Winchester diocese, ordained deacon. [*AO* (Welstead)]

797 Thomas Gerrard, B.A. (Christ Church, Oxf.), curate of Pimperne, Dors., ordained deacon. [*AO*]

798 Paul Glisson, B.A., Fellow of Trinity, Camb., ordained priest. [*AC*]

799 John White, B.A. (St. Alban Hall, Oxf.), curate of Hursley, Hants, ordained deacon. [*AO*]
[*and see* nos. 631, 760]

23 December 1639
[*see* no. 752]

30 December 1639
800 John Pearson,[1] M.A., prebendary of Netheravon. *Inst.* (f. 48) on the death of John Vincent; patron, the bishop. *Comp.* (334/20 f. 51) 28 Apr. 1640; sureties, John Heape, Thomas Trew. [*AC, DNB, FS, WR*, p. 340]

8 January 1640
801 John Comyn, vicar of North Moreton, Berks.[2] *Inst.* (f. 48) on the death of Gilbert Bradshaw; patron, John Ryves.

16 January 1640
[*see* no. 287]

15 February 1640
802 Edward Carpenter, S.T.B., vicar of Melksham. *Inst.* (f. 48) on the death of John Awdrey; patron, the dean of Salisbury. *Comp.* (334/20 f. 47) 19 Mar. 1640; sureties, Peter Seymour, Thomas Blagrave. [*AO, PR*][3]

1 March 1640
803 Hugh Chibnall, M.A. (Balliol, Oxf.), curate of Fugglestone, ordained deacon. [*AO*]

804 Henry Kinninmond, B.A. (Trinity, Oxf.), curate of Steeple Ashton, ordained deacon. [*AO, FS, PR*]

805 Henry Jordaine, B.A., curate of Barkham, Berks., ordained priest. [*AO, CR* p. 302]

806 Henry Hulbert, B.A. (Balliol, Oxf.), curate of Wootton Bassett, ordained deacon. [*AO*]
[*and see* nos. 600. 744, 767, 770]

2 March 1640
807 William Ogstone, D.D., vicar of Somerford Keynes. *Inst.* (f. 48) on the

---

[1] Son of Robert Pearson, prebendary 1626–9: nos. 256, 785.
[2] See no. 127 n.
[3] Carpenter signed the 'Concurrent Testimony' in 1648: *V.C.H. Wilts.* vii. 107.

death of John Sande; patron, the Crown. [*PR*]
[*and see* no. 563]

3 March 1640
808 William Maxwell, M.A., vicar of Warminster. *Inst.* (f. 49) on the cession of John Rogers; patron, the bishop. *Comp.* (334/20 f. 47) 31 Mar. 1640; sureties, George Thomason, Thomas Massie. [*PR, WR*]

24 March 1640
809 Richard Pugh, B.A., vicar of Aldbourne. No institution.[1] *Comp.* (334/20 f. 59) 30 June 1640; sureties, Thomas Nash, James Poole. [*AO*]
[*and see* no. 563]

25 March 1640
810 Robert Browne, M.A., vicar of Sutton Benger. *Inst.* (f. 49) on the resignation of William Noble; patron, the bishop. [? *ACO, PR*]

21 April 1640
811 Ellis Roberts, M.A., vicar of Sherston Parva *alias* Pinkney. *Inst.* (f. 49); patron, the Crown. [*AO, PR*]

28 April 1640
812 Edmund Leigh, S.T.B., rector of South Moreton, Berks. *Inst.* (f. 49) on the death of Richard Anyan; patron, John Hulloway. *Comp.* (334/20 f. 55) 18 May 1640; sureties, Charles Holloway, John Hopkins. [*AO*]

5 May 1640
[*see* no. 390]

10 June 1640
[*see* no. 665]

10 July 1640
[*see* no. 125]

16 July 1640
[*see* no. 594]

5 August 1640
[*see* no. 225]

19 August 1640
[*see* no. 563]

19 September 1640
[*see* no. 336]

---

[1] Pugh and John Rogers apparently exchanged the rectory of Compton Bassett and the vicarage of Aldbourne in 1640: cf. nos. 563, 809. The record of an institution of Rogers to the vicarage 24 Mar. is almost certainly erroneous. Rogers's name was clearly entered in mistake for Pugh's.

21 October 1640
813 Nicholas Egleton, M.A., vicar of Stratfield Mortimer, Berks. No subscription.[1] *Inst.* (f. 49) on the death of Robert Anton; patron, Eton College. [*AO*]

28 October 1640
[*see* no. 749]

12 October 1669
814 William Morse, B.A., licensed to practise medicine in the diocese.

24 September 1671
815 William Trussell, M.A.[2]

25 September 1671
816 John Hinde, ordained deacon. [*AO*]

[1] The last recorded subscription before Davenant is dated 5 Aug. 1640.
[2] The occasion for the subscription is not specified.

INDEX

References other than those preceded by 'p.' are to the entry numbers. Places other than major towns may be presumed to be in Wiltshire unless otherwise identified. Apart from peers and those in the higher ecclesiastical offices people are identified by office, rank, or occupation only when their forenames and initials are unknown or when there are two people of the same surname and forename. Peers and bishops are indexed under their surnames whether or not the surnames are given in the entries.

Mason—*cont.*
  John, 392
  Thomas, 374
  Thomas, rector of Manningford Abbots,
    34, 134
Massie, Thomas, 636, 808
Masters, James, 520
Matkin (Mackyn), Francis, 271
Maton:
  Leonard, 145
  Robert, 478
Matthew (Matthewe), Thomas, 8, 462
Mattocks, Richard, 222
Maxwell, William, 808
May, Edward, 179
Mayle, Richard, 617
Medlam, Percy, 124
Medlicott, James, 514
Meeth, John, 390
Melcombe Bingham, Dors., 189
Melksham, 244, 449, 642, 802
Membry, Christopher, 226
Mercer:
  David, 370
  Francis, 319
Mere, 307
Meredithe, Edward, 134
Meremonth, John, 749
Merick, Robert, 91, 595
Merton, Thomas, 381
Mervin (Mervyn):
  Christopher, 658
  George, 122
  Richard, 122, 437
  Thomas, 437
Michael (Michaell), John, 667
Michell (Mitchell), Samuel, 268, 557
Middleton, Thomas, 102, 195
Midgham (in Thatcham), Berks., 744
Mildenhall, 373
Miles, Henry, 616
Miller:
  Edward, 495
  Wolstan, 386
Millett, John, 375
Milton, Berks., 40
Minety, 289, 305
Minor Pars Altaris, *see* Salisbury cathedral:
  prebends
Mitchell, *see* Michell
Mogg, William, 764
Monteney, Thomas, 161
Mony, Richard, 219
Moon, William, 28
Moore (More):
  Francis, 652
  Henry, 255

Moore—*cont.*
  John, 654
  Thomas, 274, 353
  William, 37
  William, vicar of Compton, 72
Moorhouse, Lancelot, 122
More, *see* Moore
Moreton, North, Berks., 127, 801
Moreton, South, Berks., 676, 812
Morgan, Thomas, 289, 305, 307
Morland:
  Martin, 102
  Thomas, 102, 220
Morris, George, 426
Morse:
  William, 44, 556, 575
  William, physician, 814
Mosely, (Moseley), John, 743
Munden, Henry, 111
Mundy (Mundey):
  Francis, 788
  George, 532
Myhell, John, 453

Nash, Thomas, 809
Nayle, Samuel, 136
Neate, Anthony, 15, 356
Nelson, Thomas, 405
Netheravon, *see* Salisbury cathedral: pre-
  bends
Netherbury, Dors., *see* Salisbury cathedral:
  prebends
Netherhampton (in Wilton), 186
Nettleton, 137, 662
Neville (Nevill, Newill):
  Sir Henry, 261, 329
  Richard, 455 n.
Newbury:
  Humphrey, 329, 337, 455 n.
  Humphrey [? another], 455
Newbury, Berks., 19, 525
Newby, John, 322
Newill, *see* Neville
Newley, Joseph, 440
Newman:
  Jerome, 63
  John, 78
Newnton, North, 606
  prebend, 307
  and see Knoyle, West
Newstead, Christopher, 352
Newton, John, 577
Newton (in Buckland), Berks., 334
Newton, South, 409
Newton Tony, 503
Newton Valence, Hants, 770

Seymour—*cont.*
  William, 208
  William, earl of Hertford, 361
Shaffard, William, 194
Shaftesbury, Dors.:
  Holy Trinity, 146 n.
  St. Laurence's, 146
Shalbourne, formerly partly Berks., p. 3;
    626
Shapley (Shepley, Shipley), Bartholomew,
    336, 406
Sharpe:
  John, curate of Porton, 666
  John, prebendary of Horningsham and
    Tytherington, 180
  Lionel, 127
Shasbrook, *see* Shottesbrook
Shaw, Berks., 263, 761
Sheaf (Sheafe):
  Grindall, 640
  Thomas, 788
Shearce, Francis, 137
Sheldon:
  Edward, 93
  Gilbert, 466, 471, 490
Shellingford, Berks., 763
Shepherd, *see* Sheppard
Shepley, *see* Shapley
Sheppard (Shepherd), Nicholas, 730
Sherfeld (Sherfield):
  Edward, 128
  Henry, 36, 128
  Robert, 128
  Roger, 128
Sherfield English, Hants, 233
Sherrington, William, 391
Sherrington, 402
Sherston Magna, 749
Sherston Parva (Pinkney), 811
Shinfield, Berks., 506
Shipley, *see* Shapley
Shipton, John, 102
Shipton, Oxon., *see* Salisbury cathedral:
    prebends
Shorncote, Glos., formerly Wilts., 24,
    787
Shottesbrook (Shasbrook), Berks., 51, 65,
    674
Shrewton, 656
Shroton, *see* Iwerne Courtnay
Shute, William, 286
Shuter, Thomas, p. 6
Sidenham, Bampfield, 595
Simpson (Simpsion, Symson):
  SEdward, 107
  Robert, 422
  Thomas, 401

Singleton:
  John, 8
  Thomas, 33
Skeate, John, 170
Skinner:
  Thomas, 537
  William, 527
Slade:
  Francis, 70
  John, 268
  Jordan, 355
Slater:
  Edmund, 52
  Ralph, 274
Smallwood, William, 794
Smart (Smarte):
  Thomas, curate of Castle Eaton, 357
  Thomas, vicar of Eisey, 93
Smith (Smythe):
  Daniel, 701
  Henry, 279
  Humphrey, curate of Little Somerford,
    723
  Humphrey, vicar of Eisey, 93, 120
  John, 548
  John, curate of St. Lawrence's, Reading,
    85
  John, of St. Mary Hall, Oxf., 83, 548
  John patron of Liddington, 575
  John,, *alias* Howell, 61, 79
  Matthew, 508
  Nathan, 749
  Nathaniel, 679
  Nicholas, 270
  Richard, 575
  Robert, 59
  Thomas, 188
  William, 120, 296
  and see Howell
Snead, John, 787
Sneele (Snell), John, 24
Solemn League and Covenant, p. 2
Some, Benjamin, 626
Somerford [*unspecified*], 623
Somerford, Great, 571, 602, 677
Somerford, Little, 723
Somerford Keynes, Glos., formerly Wilts.,
    807
Somerset, *see* Bedminster; Brean; Dun-
    wear; Lovington; Wadeford
Sompner, William, 514
Sonning, Berks., 494, 679
Sopworth, 128, 212, 725
Sorrel, William, 536
South:
  Anthony, 43
  Francis, 39

WILTSHIRE RECORD SOCIETY

(As at 1 November 1976)

President: PROFESSOR RALPH B. PUGH, D. LIT.
Honorary Editor: D. C. COX
Honorary Treasurer: MICHAEL J. LANSDOWN
Honorary Secretary: MRS. NANCY D. STEELE

Committee:
C. E. BLUNT, O.B.E., F.B.A.
MRS. HELEN M. BONNEY
K. H. ROGERS
MISS S. ROOKE
MISS ELIZABETH CRITTALL (*co-opted*)
RICHARD E. SANDELL, representing the Wiltshire Archaeological
and Natural History Society

Honorary Auditor: MAURICE G. RATHBONE

Correspondent for the U.S.A.: CHARLES P. GOULD

PRIVATE MEMBERS

ANDERSON, D. M., 64 Winsley Road, Bradford-on-Avon
APPLEGATE, Miss Jean M., 55 Holbrook Lane, Trowbridge
AVERY, Mrs. Susan, 21 High Street, Downton

BADENI, The Countess, Norton Manor, Malmesbury
BAKER, M., 73 Easton Royal, Pewsey
BERRETT, A. M., 65 Mandeville Road, Southgate, London N14
BIDDULPH, G. M. R., c/o Personnel Records British Council, 65 Davies Street, London W1
BIRLEY, N. P., D.S.O., M.C., Hyde Leaze, Hyde Lane, Marlborough
BLAKE, T. N., 16 West Hill Road, London SW18
BLUNT, C. E., O.B.E., F.B.A., Ramsbury Hill, Ramsbury, Marlborough
BONNEY, Mrs. H. M., Flint Cottage, Netton, Salisbury
BOULTER, E. J., The School House, 34 West Street, Wilton
BRANDWOOD, K., 199 Kirkstall Lane, Leeds

BRICE, G. R., Branchways, Willett Way, Petts Wood, Kent
BRIGGS, Miss M., Glebe Cottage, Middle Woodford, Salisbury
BROOKE-LITTLE, J. P., M.V.O., Richmond Herald of Arms, College of Arms, Queen Victoria Street, London EC4
BROWN, W. E., The Firs, Beckhampton, Marlborough
BRYE, The Comtesse de, Boyton Manor, Warminster
BUCKERIDGE, J. M., 104 Beacon Road, Loughborough, Leics.
BURGE, S. F. M., The Old Rectory, Huish, Marlborough
BURGESS, J. M., Aramco 61552, P.O. Box 404, Abqaiq, Saudi Arabia
BURNETT BROWN, Miss Janet M., Lacock Abbey, Chippenham
BUXTON, E. J. M., Cole Park, Malmesbury

CALLEY, Sir Henry, D.S.O., D.F.C., D.L. Overtown House, Wroughton, Swindon
CANNING, Capt. J. B., 51212 Wall, Spokane, Wash., 99204, USA
CAREW-HUNT, Miss P. H., Cowleaze, Edington, Westbury

CARTER, Miss N. M. G., Gatehouse, Cricklade

CAVE, W. E., Everleigh, Marlborough

CHURN, R., 5 Veritys, Hatfield, Herts.

CLANCHY, M. T., Dept. of History, The University, Glasgow W2

CLARK, J. W., Manor Farm, Etchilhampton, Devizes

CODRINGTON, Miss N. E., Wroughton House, Swindon

COLLINS, W. Greville, Luckington Manor, Chippenham

COOMBES-LEWIS, R. J., 18 Bishopthorpe Road, London SE26

COX, D. C., 9 Mount Way, Pontesbury, Shrewsbury

COX, Miss P. M., 6 Silverbeech Avenue, Liverpool

CRITTALL, Miss Elizabeth, 16 Downside Crescent, London NW3

CROWLEY, D. A., 333 Cranbrook Road, Ilford, Essex

CUFFE-ADAMS, E.J., Merryfield, St. George's Road, Bickley, Bromley, Kent

DANIELS, C. G., 81 Goffenton Drive, Oldbury Court, Fishponds, Bristol

D'ARCY, J. N., Monkswell Cottage, Edington, Westbury

DAWNAY, Capt. O. P., Wexcombe House, Marlborough

DEDMAN, The Revd. S. C., The Rectory, Great Wishford, Salisbury

DIBBEN, A. A., 18 Clare Road, Lewes, East Sussex

DOYLE, Leslie, Cheviot, Clay Lane, Wythenshawe, Manchester 23

DYETT, B.T., 72 Douglas Avenue, Exmouth, Devon

DYKE, P. J., 35 Buckleigh Avenue, Merton Park, London SW20

EAST, A., The Hollow, Homington, Salisbury

EGAN, T. M., Vale Cottage, Stert, Devizes

ELKINS, T. W., 42 Brookhouse Road, Cove, Farnborough, Hants

ELRINGTON, C. R., Institute of Historical Research, University of London, Senate House, London WC1

FLOWER-ELLIS, J. G. K., Skogshogskolan, S104 05, Stockholm 50, Sweden

FORBES, Miss K. G., Bury House, Codford, Warminster

FOY, J. D., 28 Penn Lea Road, Bath, Som.

FRY, Mrs. P. M., 18 Pulteney Street, Bath, Som.

FULLER, Maj. Sir Gerard, Bt. Neston Park, Corsham

GHEY, J. G., 1 Sandell Court, The Parkway, Bassett, Southampton

GIBBON, The Revd. Canon Geoffrey, 1 North Grove, London N6

GIBBONS, M. E., 11 Fleetwood Close, Neston, Corsham

GILBERT, Mrs. V., 68 Sturges Road, Wokingham, Berks.

GIMSON, H. M., Grey Wethers, Stanton St. Bernard, Marlborough

GINGELL, Miss B., 1 Homefield, Church Lane, Godstone, Surrey

GODDARD, Mrs. G.H., The Boot, Scholard's Lane, Ramsbury, Marlborough

GOUGH, Miss P., 7 Shenstone Close, Bromsgrove, Worcs.

GOULD, C. P., 1200 Old Mill Road, San Marino, Calif., 91108, USA

HALLWORTH, Frederick, Northcote, Westbury Road, Bratton, Westbury

HAMILTON, Capt. R., West Dean, Salisbury

HANCOCK, J., Flat 25, 24 Islip Street, London SW1

HARFIELD, Maj. A. G., Royal Brunei Malay Regiment, Berakes Camp, State of Brunei, B.F.P.O. 605

HARFIELD, Mrs. A. G., Royal Brunei Malay Regiment, Berakes Camp, State of Brunei, B.F.P.O. 605

HATCHWELL, R. C., The Old Rectory, Little Somerford, Chippenham

HAWKINS, M. J., 121 High Street, Lewes, Sussex

HEMBRY, Mrs. P. M., 24 Thorncliffe, Lansdown Road, Cheltenham

HILLMAN, R. B., 38 Parliament Street, Chippenham

HOBBS, Miss N., 140 Western Road, Sompting, Lancing, Sussex

HOPE, Robert, 25 Hengistbury Road, Bournemouth

HUMPHREYS, Cdr. L. A., R.N.(Rtd.), Elm Lodge, Biddestone, Chippenham

HURSTFIELD, Prof. Joel, D.Lit., 7 Glenilla Road, London NW3

IMREDY, Mrs. D. M., 2132 Yew Street, Vancouver, B.C., Canada

JACKSON, R. H., 17 Queens Road, Tisbury, Salisbury

JEACOCK, D., 2 The Rope Yard, Wootton Bassett.

JELLICOE, The Right Hon. The Earl, D.S.O., M.C., Tidcombe Manor, Tidcombe, Marlborough

JENNER, D. A., 98 Prince's Avenue, London, NW5

JONES, The Revd. Kingsley C., Wollaston Vicarage, Middletown, Welshpool, Powys

KEATINGE, The Lady, Teffont, Salisbury

KEMPSON, E. G. H., Sun Cottage, Hyde Lane, Marlborough

KING, A. M., South Lodge, 79 Glen Eyre Road, Bassett, Southampton

KINROSS, J. S., Leigh's Green House, Corsley

KITCHING, Mrs. W. M., Willow Cottage, Pitton, Salisbury

KOMATSU, Prof. Y., Institute of European Economic History, Waseda University, Tokyo 160, Japan

LANSDOWN, M. J., 53 Clarendon Road, Trowbridge

LAURENCE, Miss Anne, 37 Denning Road, London NW5

LAURENCE, G. F., 1 Monks Orchard, Petersfield, Hants

LEETE-HODGE, Miss J. A., Tebbutts, The Breach, Devizes

LEVER, R. E., Reads Close, Teffont Magna, Salisbury

LITTLE, J. E., The Pantiles, Chapel Lane, Uffington, Berks.

LONDON, Miss V. C. M., Underholt, Westwood Road, Bidston, Birkenhead

MCCULLOUGH, Prof. Edward, Sir George Williams University, 1435 Drummond Street, Montreal 25, Que., Canada

MCGOWAN, B., 108 Dixon Street, Swindon

MACKECHNIE-JARVIS, C., 9 The Close, Salisbury

MACKINTOSH, Duncan, C.B.E., Woodfolds, Oaksey, Malmesbury

MADDEN, I. B., Rosslea, 15 Belvedere Street, Epsom, Auckland 3, N.Z.

MANN, Miss J. de L., D.Litt., The Cottage, Bowerhill, Melksham

MARGADALE, The Lord, T.D., Fonthill House, Tisbury

MERRYWEATHER, A., Frithwood Cottage, Bussage, Stroud, Glos.

MILLBOURN, Sir Eric, C.M.G., Conkwell Grange, Limpley Stoke, Bath, Som.

MITTON, A. W. D., The Dungeon, 239 Earl's Court Road, London SW5

MOODY, G. C., Montrose, Shaftesbury Road, Wilton, Salisbury

MOORE, I. G., Raycroft, Lacock, Chippenham

MORLAND, T. E., 1 Chantry Road, Wilton, Salisbury

MORRIS, Miss Bronwen, 9 Cleveland Gardens, Trowbridge

MOULTON, A. E., The Hall, Bradford-on-Avon

NAN KIVELL, R. de C., 20 Cork Street, London W1

NEWALL, R. S., Avon Cottage, Lower Woodford, Salisbury

O'GRADY, Miss C., 49 Oxford Street, Ramsbury, Marlborough

OSBORNE, Maj. Robert, 28 Munro Road, Bushey

PAFFORD, J. H. P., D.Lit., Hillside, Allington Park, Bridport, Dorset

PASKIN, Lady, Wishford, Salisbury

PERRY, S. H., 117 London Road, Kettering, Northants.

PHILLIMORE, Miss M. G., 18 Queens Street, Worthing, Sussex

PONTING, K. G., Becketts House, Edington, Westbury

POTHECARY, S. G., 41 Australian Avenue, Salisbury

PUGH, Prof. R. B., D.Lit., 67 Southwood Park, London N6

RAMSAY, G. D., 15 Charlbury Road, Oxford

RANCE, H. F., Butler's Court, Beaconsfield, Bucks.

RATHBONE, M. G., Craigleith, Snarlton Lane, Melksham Forest

RAYBOULD, Miss Frances, 20 Radnor Road, Salisbury

REEVES, Miss Marjorie E., F.B.A., 38 Norham Road, Oxford

ROGERS, K. H., Silverthorne House, East Town, West Ashton, Trowbridge

ROKEBY-THOMAS, The Revd. H. R., 4 Jackson Avenue, Kitchener, Ont., Canada, N2H, 3P1

ROOKE, Mrs. R. E. P., Old Rectory, Little Langford, Salisbury

ROOKE, Miss S. F., Old Rectory, Little Langford, Salisbury

Ross, Harry, Leighton Villa, Wellhead Lane, Westbury

Rundle, Miss Penelope, 46 St. Andrews Road, Bemerton, Salisbury

Sandell, R. E., Hillside, 64 Devizes Road, Potterne

Sandquist, Prof. T. A., Dept. of History, University of Toronto 5, Ont., Canada

Sanger, Mrs. J., 46 Woodside Road, Salisbury

Savernake Estate, Savernake Forest, Marlborough

Sawyer, L. F. T., 51 Sandridge Road, Melksham

Shadbolt, Mrs. L. G., Birkhall House, High Kelling, Holt, Norfolk

Shewring,D.G., 4 Clifton Street, Treorchy, Rhondda

Skinner, M., 19 Cheyne Court, London SW3

Smith, R. G., 142 Peabody Estate, London N17

Snow, Mrs. P. M., Westward, 240 Down Road, Portishead, Bristol

Somerset, The Duke of, D.L., Bradley House, Maiden Bradley, Warminster

Steele, Mrs. N. D., Milestones, Hatchet Close, Hale, Fordingbridge, Hants

Stevenson, Miss J. H., Institute of Historical Research, University of London, Senate House, London WC1

Stewart, Miss K. P., Moxham Villa, 57 Lower Road, Bemerton, Salisbury

Stillman, G. H., Unit 8, 10 East Street, Maylands 6051, West Australia

Stratton, J. M., Manor House Farm, Stockton, Warminster

Styles, Philip, 21 Castle Lane, Warwick

Sykes, Bonar H. C., Conock Manor, Devizes

Taylor, C. C., Royal Commission on Historical Monuments (England), 13 West End, Whittlesford, Cambridge

Turner, I. D., Warrendene, 222 Nottingham Road, Mansfield, Notts.

Turner, Miss M., 4 Elm Grove Road, Salisbury

Twine, S. W., Park Fold, 6 St. John's Way, Charlton, Malmesbury

Vernon, Miss T. E., Dyer's Leaze, Lacock, Chippenham

Warren, P., 8 Stephens Close, Harnham Meadows, Salisbury

Weinstock, Sir Arnold, Bowden Park, Lacock, Chippenham

Willan, Group Capt. F. A., D.L., Bridges, Teffont, Salisbury

Williams, N. J., 57 Rotherwick Road, Hampstead Garden Suburb, London NW11

Wiltshire, D.C.S., 17 Macaulay Buildings, Bath, Som.

Wiltshire, Julian M., 7 Lalor Street, SW6

Woodhead, Miss Barbara, 47 High Street, Ramsbury

Worthington, B. S., Vale Lodge, Colnbrook, Bucks.

Young, C. L. R., 25 Stavely Road, Chiswick, London W4

UNITED KINGDOM INSTITUTIONS

Aberdeen. King's College Library

Aberystwyth. National Library of Wales
    ,,   University College of Wales

Allington (S. Wilts.). Bourne Valley Historical Society

Bangor. University College of North Wales

Bath. General Reference Library

Birmingham. Central Public Library
    ,,   Unversity Library

Brighton. University of Sussex Library, Falmer

Bristol. City of Bristol Library
    ,,   University Library

Cambridge. University Library

Canterbury. University of Kent Library

Coventry. University of Warwick Library

Devizes. Wiltshire Archaeological and Natural History Society

Dorchester. County of Dorset Library

Edinburgh. National Library of Scotland
    ,,   University Library

Exeter. University Library

Glasgow. University Library

Gloucester. Bristol and Gloucestershire Archaeological Society

Hull. University Library

Leeds. University Library
Leicester. University Library
Liverpool. University Library
London. British Library
  ,,   College of Arms
  ,,   Guildhall Library
  ,,   Inner Temple Library
  ,,   Institute of Historical Research
  ,,   London Library
  ,,   Public Record Office
  ,,   Royal Historical Society
  ,,   Society of Antiquaries
  ,,   Society of Genealogists
  ,,   University of London Library
  ,,   Westminster Public Library
Manchester. Rylands University Library
Marlborough. Adderley Library, Marlborough College
Norwich. University of East Anglia Library
Nottingham. University Library
Oxford. Bodleian Library
  ,,   Exeter College Library
  ,,   New College Library
Reading. Central Library
  ,,   University Library

St. Andrews. University Library
Salisbury. History Dept., College of Sarum St. Michael
  ,,   Diocesan Record Office
  ,,   The Museum
  ,,   Royal Commission on Historical Monuments (England), Manor Road
  ,,   Salisbury College of Technology
Sheffield. University Library
Southampton. University Library
Swansea. University College of Swansea Library
Swindon. Swindon College Library
Taunton. Somerset Archaeological and Natural History Society
Trowbridge. Wiltshire County Library and Museum Service
  ,,   Wiltshire Record Office, County Hall
  ,,   The Wiltshire Times
York. University of York Library, Heslington

INSTITUTIONS OVERSEAS

AUSTRALIA

Adelaide. Barr Smith Library, University of Adelaide
Canberra. National Library of Australia
Melbourne. Baillieu Library, University of Melbourne
  ,,   Victoria State Library
St. Lucia, Brisbane. Main Library, University of Queensland
Sydney. Fisher Library, University of Sydney

CANADA

Downsview, Ont. Scott Library, York University
Kingston, Ont. Douglas Library, Queen's University
London, Ont. D. B. Weldon Library, University of Western Ontario
Montreal, Que. Sir George Williams University Library
Ottawa, Ont. Carleton University Library
Peterborough, Ont. Thomas J. Bata Library, Trent University
St. John's, Newf. Memorial University of Newfoundland Library

Toronto, Ont. University of Toronto Library
Vancouver, B.C. Main Library, University of British Columbia
Victoria, B.C. McPherson Library, University of Victoria

DENMARK

Copenhagen. The Royal Library

GERMANY

Göttingen. Niedersächsische Staats- und Universitätsbibliothek

REPUBLIC OF IRELAND

Dublin. National Library of Ireland
  ,,   Trinity College Library

JAPAN

Osaka. Institute of Economic History, Kansai University
Sendai. Institute of Economic History, Tohoku University

NEW ZEALAND

Wellington. National Library of New Zealand

Uppsala. Royal University Library

UNITED STATES OF AMERICA
Ann Arbor, Mich. General Library, University of Michigan
Athens, Ga. University Libraries, University of Georgia
Atlanta, Ga. The Robert W. Woodruff Library for Advanced Studies, Emory University
Baltimore, Md. George Peabody Dept., Enoch Pratt Free Library
Bloomington, Ind. Indiana University Library
Boston, Mass. Public Library of the City of Boston
  „   „   New England Historic Genealogical Society
Boulder, Colo. University of Colorado Libraries
Cambridge, Mass. Harvard Law School Library
  „   „   Harvard College Library
Chicago, Ill. University of Chicago Library
  „   „   Newberry Library
Cleveland, Ohio. Public Library
De Kalb, Ill. Northern University of Illinois, Swen Franklin Parson Library
East Lansing, Mich. Michigan State University Library
Eugene, Oreg. University of Oregon Library
Evanston, Ill. Garrett-Seabury Western Theological Libraries
Fort Wayne, Ind. Public Library of Fort Wayne and Allen County
Hattiesburg, Miss. University of Southern Mississippi Library

Haverford, Pa., Haverford College Library,
Iowa City, Iowa. State University of Iowa Library
Ithaca, N.Y. Cornell University Library
Las Cruces, N. Mex. New Mexico State University Library
Los Angeles, Calif. Public Library of Los Angeles
  „   „   „   University Research Library, University of California
Minneapolis, Ma. Dept. of History, Minnesota University
Newark, Del. University of Delaware Library
New Brunswick, N.J. Rutgers State University Library
New Haven, Conn. Yale University Library
New York, N.Y. Columbia University of the City of New York
  „   „   „   Public Library, City of New York
Notre Dame, Ind. Notre Dame University Memorial Library
Philadelphia, Pa. Pennsylvania University Library
Princeton, N.J. Princeton University Library
Salt Lake City, Utah. Genealogical Society of the Church of Latter Day Saints
San Marino, Calif. Henry E. Huntington Library
Santa Barbara, Calif. University of California Library
South Hadley, Ma. Mount Holyoke College Library
Stanford, Calif. Stanford University Library
Urbana, Ill. University of Illinois Library
Washington, D.C. Library of Congress
  „   „   Folger Shakespeare Library
Winston-Salem, N.C. Wake Forest University Library

LIST OF PUBLICATIONS

The Wiltshire Record Society was founded in 1937, as the Records Branch of the Wiltshire Archaeological and Natural History Society, to promote the publication of the documentary sources for the history of Wiltshire. The annual subscription is £4.50p. In return, a member receives a volume each year. Prospective members should apply to Mrs. N. D. Steele, Milestones, Hatchet Close, Hale, Fordingbridge, Hants. Many more members are needed.

The following volumes have been published. Price to members £4.50p and to non-members £7, postage extra. Available from the Hon. Treasurer, Mr. M. J. Lansdown, 53 Clarendon Road, Trowbridge, Wiltshire.

XXVII *Wiltshire returns to the bishop's visitation queries, 1783.* Edited by Mary Ransome (1972). Folder

XXVIII *Wiltshire extents for debts Edward I-Elizabeth I.* Edited by Angela Conyers (1973)

XXIX *Abstracts of feet of fines relating to Wiltshire for the reign of Edward III.* Edited by C. R. Elrington (1974)

XXX *Abstracts of Wiltshire tithe apportionments.* Edited by R. E. Sandell (1975)

XXXI *Poverty in early-Stuart Salisbury.* Edited by Paul Slack (1976)

VOLUMES IN PREPARATION

Wiltshire glebe terriers, edited by Susan Avery; *The charters of Lacock Abbey,* edited by K. H. Rogers; *The Edington cartulary,* edited by Janet Stevenson; *Dean Chaundler's register,* edited by T. C. B. Timmins; *The Bradenstoke cartulary,* edited by Vera C. M. London; *Wiltshire gaol delivery and trailbaston trials 1275-1306,* edited by R. B. Pugh

A leaflet giving fuller details may be obtained from Mrs. Steele, Milestones, Hatchet Close, Hale, Fordingbridge, Hants.